ROCK CLIMBING

Greenwood Guides to Extreme Sports

Surfing: The Ultimate Guide
Douglas Booth

Snowboarding: The Ultimate Guide
Holly Thorpe

BASE Jumping: The Ultimate Guide
Jason Laurendeau

ROCK CLIMBING
The Ultimate Guide

Victoria Robinson

GREENWOOD GUIDES TO EXTREME SPORTS
Holly Thorpe and Douglas Booth, Series Editors

AN IMPRINT OF ABC-CLIO, LLC
Santa Barbara, California • Denver, Colorado • Oxford, England

Library of Congress Cataloging-in-Publication Data

Robinson, Victoria.
    Rock climbing : the ultimate guide / Victoria Robinson.
        p. cm. — (Greenwood guides to extreme sports)
    Includes bibliographical references and index.
    ISBN 978–0–313–37861–4 (hard copy : alk. paper) — ISBN 978–0–313–37862–1 (ebook)
1. Rock climbing. I. Title.
GV200.2.R65   2013
796.522'3—dc23   2012031304

ISBN: 978–0–313–37861–4
EISBN: 978–0–313–37862–1

17 16 15 14 13   1 2 3 4 5

This book is also available on the World Wide Web as an eBook.
Visit www.abc-clio.com for details.

Greenwood
An Imprint of ABC-CLIO, LLC

ABC-CLIO, LLC
130 Cremona Drive, P.O. Box 1911
Santa Barbara, California 93116-1911

This book is printed on acid-free paper ∞

Manufactured in the United States of America

For Fast Eddie

contents

series foreword

of interest to students and enthusiasts alike, extreme sports are recharging and redefining athletics around the world. While baseball, soccer, and other conventional sports typically involve teams, coaches, and an extensive set of rules, extreme sports more often place the individual in competition against nature, other persons, and themselves. Extreme sports have fewer rules, and coaches are less prominent. These activities are often considered to be more dangerous than conventional sports, and that element of risk adds to their appeal. They are at the cutting edge of sports and are evolving in exciting ways.

While extreme sports are fascinating in their own right, they are also a window on popular culture and contemporary social issues. Extreme sports appeal most to the young, who have the energy and daring to take part in them, and who find in them an alternative culture with its own values and vocabulary. At the same time, surfing and various other extreme sports have long histories and are important to traditional cultures around the world. The extreme versions of these sports sometimes employ enhanced technology or take place under excessively challenging conditions. Thus they build on tradition yet depart from it. Extreme sports are increasingly significant to the media, and corporations recognize the marketing value of sponsoring them. Thus extreme sports become linked with products, their star athletes become celebrities, and their fans are exposed to a range of media messages. Local governments might try to regulate skateboarding and other extreme activities, sometimes out of safety concerns and sometimes out of moral ones. Yet other communities provide funding for skateboard parks, indoor rock climbing facilities, and other venues for extreme sports enthusiasts. Thus extreme sports become part of civil discourse.

Designed for students and general readers, this series of reference books maps the world of extreme sports. Each volume looks at a particular sport and includes information about the sport's history, equipment and techniques, and important players. Volumes are written by professors or other authorities and are informative, entertaining, and engaging. Students using these books learn about sports that interest them and discover more about cultures, history, social issues, and trends. In doing so, they become better prepared to engage in critical assessments of extreme sports in particular and of society in general.

Holly Thorpe and Douglas Booth, Series Editors

preface

in the winter of 1994, late at night, I found myself standing with the British climber Colin Gibberd on the main street of North Conway, New Hampshire. At the time, I was also pregnant with our son, Eddie Joe Robinson. We had not arranged any accommodation beforehand but had ventured here "on spec" from England via New York, on a Greyhound bus, to ice climb at Cathedral Ledge and Mount Washington. We went into a nearby garage and began talking to a local man who was staying at a ski lodge in the town. When he realized I was pregnant, he offered us, as he put it, "a room at the inn." We went ice climbing and stayed in the Harvard Cabin on Mount Washington. As I recall, I also made my first Betty Crocker cake on this trip as a thank you to those people who had shown us such kindness and hospitality. A man who was staying at the ski lodge informed us both that because of the extremely adverse weather conditions, "you *will* die" when we told him we were going ice climbing on Mount Washington. However, all three of us survived to tell the tale.

I started climbing in the mid-1980s. This experience has included traditional climbing, sport climbing, and bouldering on rock and ice in England, Scotland, and Wales; Europe, for example, France and Spain; and the United States, where I have climbed with both male partners and friends of both sexes. After the birth of my son, and with my career as a sociologist in British universities taking off, my climbing activities ceased and I referred to myself as a "lapsed" climber. I contented myself with merely writing about the sport of rock climbing rather than practicing it. However, in 2011, I found myself sport climbing in Thailand, at Krabi, where I again realized just why climbing is such an exhilarating, pleasurable, and life-affirming sport. I do not know if or how seriously I will take up rock climbing again. Yet one thing is for certain: there is no such thing as a "lapsed climber," only one who needs sufficient sun, sand, and endless limestone crags to discover a renewed enthusiasm for the sport.

In my study of British rock climbers (Robinson, 2008), I conducted one of the first empirical studies of rock climbers in the United Kingdom when I interviewed 47 male and female climbers. These ranged from those climbers who are world class and are, or have been, at the top of the sport, to those who only go climbing on the weekend for fun or to keep fit. My focus here, as a sociologist, was on gender relations and masculinity in particular. I was specifically interested in talking to climbers about their sporting identity, how the sport has changed since more women were coming into the sport, and what men felt about their climbing abilities, bodies, and partner or family responsibilities as they got older. Their attitude to risk was also important here. I found that whether climbers are classed as elite or non-elite, a climbing identity can still be absolutely central to how they define themselves as a person.

Through participant observation, I was also able to observe a number of the interviewees in different sporting and social situations, which included interacting with them while climbing, in the outdoors and indoors, as well as in social situations. For instance, I observed participants at parties where large numbers of climbers were gathered or in other social settings such as bars or climbing and mountaineering events and conferences. In addition, my personal knowledge of some of the climbers allowed me access to their lives in the private sphere of the home—where, for instance, I could observe them with female partners or male, non-climbing friends. This was important to be able to see how sporting identities are informed and shaped by people's roles in the domestic arena. It was also useful in facilitating my being able to "get at" climbers' embodied sporting practices, which an interview itself may not always illuminate, given, as the sociologist Bourdieu (1977) points out, that much of practice is not carried out consciously. Therefore, though I would certainly not describe myself as an elite climber, my experience of rock climbing over the years and my theoretical interest in the sport have informed the writing of this book.

In writing the book, I came to realize that there is, quite possibly, nowhere on this planet which offers such diverse climbing experiences to either the fledgling or very experienced rock climber as the United States. Climbing author Mellor (2001) imagines what images French climbers would conjure up if asked to describe American climbing:

Some will see the familiar lineup of the Teton Range, the most photographed mountains in America. Others will envision the odd volcanic plug of Devil's Tower jutting above the Wyoming plains, its fluted sides lined with vertical cracks, each a climbing route. Still others will think of the huge gray walls of Yosemite's El Capitan and Half Dome, vertical crack climbing so daunting to European pocket pullers. Mention American rock climbing and some will see the stark red towers of Utah's canyon country, its eerie silences echoing even in the imagination; still others will think of the northeastern hardwood forests exploding into color beneath historic crags like the Gunks or Cathedral Ledge. (2001, 11–12)

In exploring this claim of the uniqueness of the vast American landscape for the sport of climbing, the book opens with the "Explanations" chapter, which outlines different types of climbing and looks at gender, risk, and the increasing globalization and commercialization of extreme sports in general and climbing in particular. The "Origins" chapter is concerned with the diverse roots of the United States' contemporary climbing scene through a focus on three historically important climbing areas: the "Gunks," Yosemite, and Colorado. The next chapter, "Science," explores the geology of the rock, early attempts by surveyors to plot the mountainous terrain, and the science of climbing techniques, performance, and injury. In Chapter 4, "Places and Events," current climbing activities in more established climbing areas such as the three regions discussed in Chapter 1, along with more recent hot spots for specific types of climbing, are explored. In Chapter 5, "Heroes," past and present rock climbers from the United States and abroad who have inspired and influenced others and courted controversy are highlighted. The "Technicalities" chapter discusses the technology and purpose of different kinds of climbing gear and equipment as well as the development of indoor climbing and climbing competitions. Finally, Chapter 7, "Futures," points to future trends and developments in the sport of rock climbing.

Given its focus, the book is primarily concerned with rock climbing in the United States, as opposed to ice climbing or mountaineering, though both are mentioned here at times. The focus is also on climbing in the United States and not primarily in other countries. However, given the global nature of the sport, climbing elsewhere is included for purposes of comparison or for further information, for example if a country has been influential on developments in the United States.

In writing this book, a number of people have both encouraged me and given theoretical advice or told me about relevant source materials. These include the British climber John Fleming, British climber and editor Geoff

Birtles, British climber and president of the British Mountaineering Council Rab Carrington, and the U.S. academic and climber Mike Vause. A special thank you for their detailed comments on my work goes to the well-known British climber and academic Andrew Popp; the American climber, writer, and teacher Kaydee Summers, living in Utah; and the Texan climber Karen Ghiselli (currently residing in Sheffield, England, despite the weather, so she is close to the gritstone). My editor, Holly Thorpe, has been a fantastic help in editing the manuscript and in making very helpful suggestions. Finally, I am, as always, indebted to Colin Gibberd for introducing me to the sport and taking me on my most memorable climbing adventures, and to Fast Eddie Joe Robinson, who survived Mount Washington to grow into a son we could be proud of.

1. explanations

I wanted to smell the rope and let the memories that inhabited those smells bring to me the beauty of climbing and all that was good to breathe among the rocks, timber, and air. I wanted to find ways not to have to work at some regular job. I wanted to fulfill a vision of uniqueness my mother had of me. I hoped to be able to do something that would honor, if not impress, my father. . . . I hoped to excel at climbing, because if I did I would like myself and people would like me. Of most importance, I wanted to be with a friend and share something sacred, beautiful, and ours alone.

(Ament, 2002a, 133)

extreme sports in general, and rock climbing in particular, have been defined as being less about competition, status, and bravado than other sports and are supposedly more individualistic, potentially less gendered, and likely to reveal cooperation between participants. Such sports are usually nonaggressive activities, though they can embrace risk and danger. They are usually individualistic in form or attitude and predominantly white, middle class, and Western in formation (Robinson, 2008; Wheaton, 2007). However, there are differences among some extreme sports in relation to the participants engaging with real danger or life-threatening activities, as can be the case in rock climbing.

A number of these activities—for example, snowboarding, windsurfing, and ultimate Frisbee—are newer sports; others, such as rock climbing, have a long and diverse history; others still—such as surfing—have been revitalized with new generations taking up the sport. These sports are organized around the consumption of new objects such as bikes and boards and involve new technology (for example, in rock climbing, there is new and improved gear such as climbing boots using sticky rubber to give a better grip on the rock, safer and stronger climbing harnesses, and new protection devices).

There are debates both in sociology and in the popular media, as well as among extreme sports enthusiasts in general, over which term best describes such sports. Wheaton (2004) uses the term "life style sports"; "whizz sports" is preferred by Midol and Boyar (1995); Lyng (1990; 2005) uses the term "edgework" to describe a number of diverse, high-risk activities including sport, and these are seen as sites where norms and boundaries are transgressed. Other terms used include "risk sports," "panic sports," "alternative sports," or "new" sports (see also Laviolette, 2007). "Extreme sports" is the term used by the Americans Rinehart and Sydnor (2003) for describing different sports, including climbing, in the United States and more globally. I also use this term in relation to the UK rock-climbing scene (Robinson, 2008), though there are arguments that the media has deradicalized these sports through terming them "extreme."

In addition, climbers are often perceived by nonclimbing friends and family to be obsessed with their sport, with a public perception of climbers, especially mountaineers, as being driven to reach a goal or a summit at all costs. The media can reflect and help create this view of rock climbers and mountaineers. But climbers can reject these labels and so support Rinehart and Sydnor's (2003) view that extreme sports athletes are not "lunatics" or "daredevils" but "meticulous performers, giving themselves to some lofty art form" (12).

Distinctions have been made between extreme, alternative, or lifestyle sports and more traditional sports such as football or athletics, which can be characterized as mainstream or as dominant (Robinson, 2008). Rock climbing, in comparison, has been seen as antimainstream. It is a sport that attracts the individualistic, or even the maverick, as the U.S. climber Ament's quote that opened this chapter reveals. However, theoretical approaches that have attempted to characterize extreme and traditional sports as being about either cooperation *or* competition respectively are flawed in that they often ignore variations within the sporting culture (Booth & Thorpe, 2007). Climbing, for example, can be an incredibly competitive sport for some and a recreational family weekend activity for others. Further, this polarization fails to take into account the dynamic experiences of specific individuals across their life course. Indeed, for many climbers, their motivation, skill, and commitment levels change during different phases of their lives. It is also important to note that many extreme sport participants do not necessarily reject traditional sports; many climbers also enjoy other sports such as tennis, cycling, or running.

Groups of extreme- or alternative-sports activists have also been keen to differentiate themselves from each other. For example, Browne (2004), discussing extreme-sports activists such as skaters, bikers, and boarders, notes that the "riders" did not like being lumped together "with stunt acts and freaks, not to mention skydivers, bungee jumpers or rock climbers" (11).

This can partially be explained by the need some extreme sporting participants have to maintain an authenticity about their particular sport or to argue that *their* sport is the most dangerous or risky or special. In relation to climbing, Bisharat (2010a) maintains, "Climbing is the greatest sport on earth because this vertical journey holds uncanny parallels to the scope and depth of life itself. Though I will say that a climber's life can be replete with even greater, more powerful affirmations and traumas. Therefore, climbing must be taken as seriously as life—which is best done when taken not seriously at all" (para. 2).

Furthermore, it is the relationship of climbing to the mainstream that can help explain such a position expressed by some climbers. According to sport sociologist Peter Donnelly (2003),

> The resilience and significance of climbing lies in the fact that it existed for so long as an alternative to mainstream sport, as an unincorporated and self-governing parallel to the dominant sport culture. And climbers have, in recent years, been very conscious of the difference from other sports and have acted to maintain that difference. (127)

This chapter defines different climbing styles and related developments in the sport. It then discusses the reasons why people climb, with a particular focus on identity construction. This is followed by an examination of the commercialization of climbing and the effect this has had on climbing identities and on the fragmentation within the culture. Following this discussion of difference within and among climbers is a discussion of gender and climbing and, lastly, the notion of "risk." These issues allow both historical and contemporary perspectives on major debates and controversies in the sport of rock climbing to be raised.

climbing styles

Rock climbing as a sport is very diverse in terms of the styles and activities it encompasses. Traditional climbing, using ropes, involves placing protection into cracks in the rock to allow an ascent to be made. This "leader-placed" protection is taken out by the second climber when he or she attempts to climb the route. This type of climbing also involves a "belayer" (often the second climber) who holds the ropes of the person who is leading the climb, paying the rope out. The belayer holds the rope tight if needed so the lead climber does not fall. For top roping, the climber is protected by a belayer who is fastened safely to an anchor point at the top of the climb. For bottom roping, the person belaying is doing so from the bottom of the route (Oxlade, 2003).

"Soloing" means the rock is climbed without the aid of ropes, other protection, or a belayer. Traditional climbing can encompass short or long routes, which can be completed respectively within minutes or days—for example, with big-wall climbing. With traditional climbing, either on rock or ice, the fear is that the protection that climbers have placed themselves may not hold. Added to this is the possibility of being 20 or 30 feet above the last piece of protection placed, so falling off a route can have serious, even fatal consequences. "Mountaineering" involves longer routes and is traditionally associated with adventure, risk, and danger, with the public's

Once a climber is on belay, careful attention is required. (Adam Pastula)

imagination increasingly fuelled by global coverage of ascents of the world's highest peaks. Ice climbing is a specific type of climbing that is carried out in the traditional manner using specialized equipment. Mixed climbing is a mixture of rock and ice climbing.

Sport climbing is generally judged to be less hazardous than traditional climbing and, as a consequence, is regarded as less "pure" by some in the climbing world, as this chapter goes on to discuss. Sport climbing consists of climbing routes that have been equipped with bolts (steel rings) drilled into the rock. The lead climber clips one end of a "quickdraw" to a bolt and clips the rope into the other end. This is often done when traditional protection is not possible (Oxlade, 2003). Sport climbing has been accompanied by the appearance of artificial crags, known as climbing gyms, in many U.S. cities. Though initially conceived of as a training aid for the "real thing," there is now a whole generation of climbers who have learned to climb indoors, never having been on a rock face. This creation of an artificial climbing arena was, subsequently, followed by organized competition climbing, league tables, and, eventually, an international competition climbing circuit. (See Chapter 4, "Places and Events," for further discussion of competition climbing.)

In contrast, the practice of bouldering is a style of climbing a few feet off the ground without ropes or harnesses and using thick mats as crash pads to break falls. This form of climbing takes place indoors and outdoors. In practice, many climbers climb inside on climbing walls as a way of training to increase strength and stamina and also climb outdoors in a variety of styles.

Climbs are also graded according to their level of difficulty or how dangerous they are, with different grading systems being used in different countries for sport, traditional climbing, and bouldering. The climbing author Mellor (2001) describes the American grading system as originating at Tahquitz Rock, even though it is referred to as the Yosemite Decimal System (YDS). The American Safe Climbing Association (2003) notes that free climbs were initially rated on a closed decimal system starting from 5.0 (easiest class), then 5.1, 5.2, and so on to 5.9. However:

After many very difficult climbs accumulated in the 5.9 rating, the decimal system was "broken" in that it was no longer a decimal system, and the 5.10 rating came in to existence, followed by 5.11, 5.12, 5.13, 5.14, and now 5.15. These upper grades were further subdivided into 4 "letter grades" to further refine the rating: the suffixes

Emily Harrington practices her moves on the walls of a rock climbing club in Boulder, Colorado. (AP/Wide World Photos)

a, b, c, and d were associated with increasing difficulty (i.e. "easy 5.10" = 5.10a or 5.10b, "hard 5.10" = 5.10c or 5.10d). (American Safe Climbing Association, 2003, para. 5)

Mountaineering or big-wall climbs can also be graded for how serious or long they are. This allows climbers to further distinguish between climbs. The ratings given are also subjective. Bouldering is graded by a different system, which is normally referred to as the V grade system, which currently ranges from V1 to 16. (Though bouldering was originally assessed by John Gill's "B" system in the 1950s, this was replaced by the V system in the 1990s by John Sherman at Hueco Tanks, Texas.)

USA	UIAA	Norway	Australian	S. Africa	Sport	British Trad.
5.1	I		4	6	1	Mod
5.2	II			8	2	Diff
5.3	III	3	6	9	2+	VDiff
5.4	III+	4	8	10	3-	HVD
5.5	IV		10	11	3	Sev
5.6	IV+	4+	12	12	3+	HS
5.7	V-	5-	14	13	4	VS
5.8	V	5	16	14/15	4+	HVS
5.9	V+	5+	16	16	5	E1
5.10a	VI-	6-	18	17	5+	
5.10b	VI	6	19	18	6a	E2
5.10c	VI+		20	19	6a+	E3
5.10d	VII	6+	20	20	6b	E4
5.11a	VII+	7-	21	21	6b+	
5.11b	VIII-	7	22	22	6c	E5
5.11c	VIII-		23	23	6c+	
5.11d	VIII	7+	24	24	7a	E6
5.12a	VIII+		24	25	7a+	
5.12b	IX-	8-	25	26	7b	E7
5.12c	IX-		26	27	7b+	E8
5.12d	IX	8	27	28	7c	
5.13a	IX+	8+	28	29	7c+	E9
5.13b	X-		29	30	8a	
5.13c	X	9-	30	31	8a+	E10
5.13d	X	9	31	32	8b	
5.14a	X+		32	33	8b+	E11
5.14b	XI-	9+	33	34	8c	
5.14c	XI		34	35	8c+	
5.14d	XI+		35	36	9a	
5.15a	XI+		36	37	9a+	
5.15b	XI-		37		9b	
5.15c	XI		38		9b+	

Climbing difficulty grade comparison table. (ABC-CLIO)

There are also international differences in grading systems. For example, in Europe, different grading systems exist for sport and traditional climbs, while in the United States the same rating system is used for both sport and traditional climbs. For example, the E1–E12 system is used in the United Kingdom to grade traditional routes (easier climbs are labeled from moderate to HVS), and a sport climb is graded using a number rating of 1 through 9 with added letters a through c+ to show the risk element involved in any climb. Differences in ratings exist across Europe, for example as in France with the Fontainebleau "Font" system. The sport-grade system began in France. Currently, in the United States, the hardest route climbed, either sport or traditional, is 5.14bx (the 'x' refers to the risk/protection element of any given climb), and this would be graded 9b for a sport climb and E12 for a traditional route in the United Kingdom. Though these grades are being challenged all the time. There have been, to date, reports of the V16 grade being achieved for bouldering. The tables compiled to illustrate these grading systems do not always fully reflect the hardest grades currently being climbed. This is partially due to the achievement of such grades not always being able to be verified straight away. The grades they refer to are also open to interpretation.

Clearly, therefore, rock climbing needs to be recognized in all its different elements—traditional climbing, sport climbing, competition climbing, big-wall climbing, and soloing, for example—as a diversifying and rapidly changing sport.

why climbers climb

Sport means different things to different people. For some professional athletes it represents the routines of daily work, for others it is cathartic and stress reducing, and for many others it is a form of fun and play. Both psychological and physiological reasons contribute to the urge many climbers have to scale rocks and mountains, as I discuss later in the chapter in relation to "risk." Yet the reasons why people climb cannot be reduced to one simple explanation. For some, rock climbing can allow people to cope with modern life: "Climbing has always been a part of my life . . . no matter what life has thrown at me—bad jobs, bad relationships, bad choices. I might take a year off here or there, but I always come back" (Lynch, 2009, 11).

Sometimes, climbing is taken up in opposition to a materialistic society: "Many people wonder when they can first call themselves a 'real climber.' We live in a material society, where we've decided that the things we own say the most about who we are. If you own a harness, belay device and rock shoes, then you're a climber" (Bisharat, 2010a, para. 4).

Others proclaim that rock climbing allows them to travel to beautiful places without necessarily being a tourist. Another reason is the call of the wild: "We climbers have a bright red fire in our bellies. For wild ascents. For wild places" (Irvine, 2002, 203). Climbing is about having a strong sense of individualism but also, as one climber reveals, the camaraderie and friendships with fellow climbers:

> DP is one of my best friends. . . . DP is a perfect example of that uniquely Austin creature charitably referred to as a "slacker." Hired by an Austin climber who struck it rich in the dot com boom, DP works as a caretaker for a piece of property near Lake Travis, but mostly climbs and avoids his ex-wife who hounds him for child support. He's simultaneously one of the laziest and smartest people I've ever known. He's a great climbing partner and is endlessly entertaining, dead-panning simple yet brilliantly incongruous gems of wisdom. For example, when I asked him how he felt after spending Christmas and the next four months in jail on an assault charge that was eventually dropped he said, "In this life all you can hope for is to be stronger than the shit slamming into you." (Jackson, 2010a, paras. 25–27)

As this quote suggests, though rock climbing tends to attract those with a strong sense of individualism, there is also a strong community ethos within the climbing culture. Chuck Pratt, often regarded in the 1960s as the best off-width crack climber in the world, discussing the hard first ascent of the south face of Mount Watkins in Yosemite, with Warren Harding and Yvon Chouinard, said: "I thought of my incomparable friend Chouinard, and of our unique friendship, a friendship now shared with Warren, for we were united by a bond far stronger and more lasting than any we could find in the world below" (Pratt, 2002, 60).

a climbing identity

A climbing identity extends outward from individual needs or personal reasons for being a rock climber. Our identity allows us a location in the world and a link with the society we live in. There is also a connection between the subjective positions we inhabit and the social and cultural situations in which we place ourselves—and our sporting identity can be central to this (Woodward, 2002). A focus on identity can help illuminate some of the reasons discussed above, that climbers themselves gave, for having an intense desire to rock climb.

Identity gives us an idea of who we are and how we relate to other individuals. In the high-risk sport of rock climbing, a climber can choose to climb with others of the same or a different sex; decide to boulder, sport, or "trad" (traditional) climb; as well as decide to get involved in a local or national climbing "scene" or not be part of the scene at all. In this way, we construct an individual sporting identity that is shaped by the type of climbing we do and who we climb with. Furthermore, an individual climber's identity is a process that evolves over time.

These individual identity shifts can be seen and traced in both the personal histories of individual climbers as well as the broader historical and social context of climbing in the United States. For example, more people now climb, especially women, who climb in much greater numbers than previously. Also, shifts to aid climbing and then free climbing, as well as the developments of sport, indoor, and competition climbing, offer climbers a wider variety of options. (See Chapter 6, "Technicalities," for more on these shifts.)

> In an interview with Brady Robinson, the executive director of the American Access Fund (Young, 2009), Robinson outlines that the fund has about 15,000 members and affiliates. He makes the point that it is difficult to get an exact number of those who currently climb in the United States, but the outdoor industry experts think there are about 1.6 million climbers in the country, while hardcore enthusiasts, according to industry experts, number around half a million. Other reports estimate that the number of climbers is higher, perhaps around 9 million.

Identities can also be viewed as political, that is, negotiated in relation to the power of groups or individuals, and can potentially therefore create an "us and them" situation. This concept of "us" and "them" can be thought of in a number of ways, for instance, in relation to novices versus experienced climbers, elite climbers as opposed to non-elite, and traditional climbers versus indoor or sport climbers. Gender is also a way in which climbers primarily differentiate themselves. This can be seen when men and women climb together. This opposition can create tension and high emotions, for instance, if men perceive women climbers as not "serious" or "hard" enough, thus jeopardizing their own climbing success. Or, their female climbing partners may climb harder than they do, either to their dismay or sometimes to their delight.

> **Specialized aid climbing: This is when nylon stirrup ladders are attached onto the rock to hold the climber's weight. (Aids in the form of metal pegs, or pitons, are also used.) The climber uses the most gear in this type of climbing. Free climbing: This method of climbing is done when the climber is fastened to a rope via a harness to prevent falls. The climber uses his or her feet and hands to scale the rock. Free soloing: This method entails climbing without any ropes or gear. This type of climbing can be fatal (Jenkins, 2011).**

Identities can also be viewed as more or less authentic. This authenticity can even be related to the kind of rock that is climbed, so that those male climbers who do routes on gritstone in the north of England, for instance, have a national or even international reputation for being "hard men." In the United States, the "Vulgarians" have been awarded that particular accolade! (See Chapter 2, "Origins," for a discussion of their exploits.) Additionally, whether one trad climbs outside, in a more "extreme" environment, or sport climbs in the safe, more mundane environment of the climbing gym can also help to construct a more, or less, masculine sense of self and public sporting image. (See Robinson [2008] for a study of masculinity and identity in the UK rock-climbing culture.)

Thinking about how a climbing identity emerges can also mean thinking about how people develop their sense of self in relation to the activities they do and the people they interact with over their life course. Susan Fox Rogers (2002) writes about doing the route "Loose Woman" at the Shawangunks, which she says sparked her life-long love of climbing: "When I climb I rely on knowledge lodged in my muscles. The memory there emerges through smells or the rhythm of movement. . . . But these memories are not specific or logical, cannot account for how I got from here to there, how at the bottom of the climb I was one girl and at the top another. How twenty-two years ago I was her, and now I am me" (265).

Getting older can also make some climbers reassess the place that climbing has in their lives, something the following climber found when he had difficulty persuading climbing friends to go on a trip to Norway: "Everyone's priorities suddenly change when they approach 30" (Buchroithner, 2010, 6).

commercialization and the mainstream

Globalization can be seen to have had an increasing effect on sport. This includes the commercialization of a variety of extreme sports, including climbing. This has led to some extreme-sports enthusiasts being seen as professional athletes and is illustrated increasingly by the rigorous training regimes that many competitive rock climbers undertake (see Chapter 6, "Technicalities").

Some climbers are embracing the opportunities to develop a career as a professional, competitive climber. Yet there is an ongoing tension between an often perceived deradicalization of extreme sports such as rock climbing, through increased commercialization, professionalism, and the selling of lifestyle sports for mass consumption, and the idea of climbing as being a maverick and anticommercial "alternative" sport and lifestyle. This anti-establishment aspect to climbing, for instance, can be seen through the now infamous existence of Camp 4 in Yosemite Valley and the changes that have occurred since the 1960s: "Once the home of about a half-dozen climbing bums—people scorned by most tourists and nonclimbers—the campground sported ten times that number by 1970, and rock climbing had become a respectable activity, one that increasing numbers of park visitors paid money to do" (Roper, 1994, 13). (See Chapter 2, "Origins," for more detail on the camp to illustrate shifts from the sport's antimainstream past.)

Sociologists have outlined the worldwide dominance of an international Americanized culture. This includes the global dominance of economic and cultural flows coming from the United States. This is evidenced by the existence of multinational corporations such as McDonald's, Disney, and Coca-Cola. However, challenges to such a dominant culture are possible if an area such as sport is seen as a field in which ideologies, values, and meanings may be contested (Maguire,1999). For instance, even in the United States itself, alternative sports such as climbing can reveal how participants create their own, more local practices in opposition to more mainstream sport. Climbers may, for example, refuse to take part in competition climbing if this type of climbing is seen as too commercial and mainstream.

Rock climbers also debate developments within their sport at both local and global levels. Debates around sport climbing, for instance, have been concerned with whether and how this type of climbing is seen to disturb the inherent tension between difficulty and risk necessary for climbing to take place (Gifford, 2004). This is because sport climbing takes place on bolted routes and is a much safer activity than traditional climbing. This can be viewed as going against the spirit of adventure, which traditionally has been inherent to the sport in general. Sport climbing has also been linked to organized climbing competitions, which involve different government agencies and thus outside control. These agencies, like the UK government–funded British Mountaineering Council (BMC) or the U.S. American Alpine Club or International Mountaineering and Climbing Federation, can exert control over participants through demanding their accountability or giving material rewards, for example. With these views in mind, specifically in relation to mountaineering, Walter Bonatti, the great Italian climber, seen by some as the best alpinist of all time, said:

> From the beginning, I have taken my inspiration from traditional and classic ways of climbing, in which one measures oneself against a great mountain, and where everything about oneself—physical and emotional conditions and principles—is put to the test, and one must give all and spare nothing. Furthermore, a mountain that I define as "great" becomes particularly severe and exacting because of the limits imposed by the technical means that we have, and accept, to climb it. (Bonatti, cited in Ament, 2002a, 259)

In discussing his stance, the climber and writer Pat Ament (2002a) laments the fact that, to him, more and more climbers today are too concerned with reducing the difficulty of a climb through technology, bolts, and modern advancements in gear. Further, he feels that Bonatti's view, of accepting limitations to keep "true adventure intact," is a more authentic one in relation to many modern climbers.

However, many have now accepted climbing as a sport that can be comprised of different types of activity, including sport climbing. For a younger generation, raised on indoor climbing and competitions, these past debates about sport climbing do not have the same meaning and urgency that they once did.

These debates reveal climbing as a sport in a constant state of flux and contradiction. While some climbers strive to become professionals, the same climbers may also be intensely concerned with debating the ethics of different climbing practices. They can also have a concern for the environment in their manner of practicing the sport (see Chapter 7, "Futures," for a discussion of climbing and the environment as a crucial issue both now and for future generations of younger climbers). A question that can therefore be asked in respect of such debates is, how do climbers themselves make sense of these changes in a sport that traditionally has not been a commercial one and is in a period of rapid change?

Extreme sports such as climbing can be seen to represent superficial, even nihilistic, materialistic cultural forms, increasingly appropriated by transnational media corporations to be sold as a package to passive consumers (Wheaton, 2004). Therefore, the question could be asked whether rock climbers use such commercialism to their best advantage, and, in so doing, whether they are still able to maintain their integrity. So in exploring climbers' views we can see what this commercialization means to different groups of climbers, from those "hardcore" elite climbers, to weekend climbers, to those who are just starting out.

For instance, the issue of integrity and climbing ethics has been seen as being intimately connected to a "personal journey," as the climbing journalist Bisharat (2010a, para. 9) observes. He argues that the key moment in a climber's life is when something "clicks" regarding the "rules" that surround the sport. He emphasizes that the important thing, however, is that climbers must continue to debate these rules so debates do not dissolve into clichés.

Further, any view that lifestyle sports are becoming more appropriated by global media companies aiming to repackage active sports to passive consumers is perhaps not fully applicable to climbing, for rock climbing (as opposed to mountaineering, which is often televised) often makes a very poor, and some would say boring, spectator sport: "Simply put, the trouble with watching any kind of climbing, when you're not a climber yourself, is that once you've been exposed to the novel environment a couple of times and the initial surge of sympathetic fear and vertigo wears off, there's little about the activity that's obviously impressive" (Dornian, 2003, 283).

In this way, through debates over sport climbing, competition climbing, and climbing ethics, people's sporting identities continue to change and develop in sometimes unexpected ways. For example, increased commercialization does not necessarily mean that sponsored climbers have "sold out" or no longer love the sport. The American professional climber Joe Kinder, discussing the need to self-promote as a sponsored climber, says: "My blog gets 2,500 visitors a day. Experiencing climbing through the Internet, for some, is a bigger part of their climbing lives than actual climbing" (Kinder, 2010, 32). However, he also conveys the passion he clearly still feels for the sport and embraces the opportunities professional climbing offers for travelling the world: "Travelling is a test of character. Get out of your comfort zone. It's defining. As a climber, travelling is the greatest gift you can give yourself" (32).

So the continually changing story of individual identity and mass commercialization currently remains unfinished, as shown by the sheer scale of recent commercial developments around different extreme sports. It remains the case, however, that younger people have entered the sport due to the increased provision of indoor climbing gyms. On a larger scale, in the United Kingdom, Venture Xtreme is an extreme-sport concept that develops water, vertical, and wheel sporting facilities for extreme sports enthusiasts, as well as shopping and leisure complexes for spectators costing millions of pounds (http://www.venture-xtreme.com/). The intention is to build the United Kingdom's first National Extreme Sport Centre. Such developments necessitate a need to monitor how local sporting subcultures and their media and related industries react to these globalized trends. Globalization is a two-way process and not always a negative one for those extreme sports participants, including climbers, involved in these changes.

climbing and difference

Some extreme-sport researchers have suggested that these activities offer greater possibilities for resistance and disruption to hierarchical relationships based on traditional identifiers (for example, gender, race, and sexuality) (Wheaton, 2004). This is through, for instance, the promotion of more fluid gender identities and relationships and less emphasis on competition than in traditional, institutionalized, and competitive sports. The latter are more likely to be sites where dominant gender or sexuality relations, for example, can still be seen.

Sports such as climbing, though having a long history, can also be seen as new sports in that they have progressed, over time, in radical new ways.

New sports have the potential for liberating participants from traditional gender and other roles because of the blurred boundaries they create. Yet it appears that climbing is not exempt from discriminatory attitudes. The climber Phil Persson, in response to an article in the U.S. climbing magazine *Rock and Ice*, which linked "haughty alpinists" to "unrealized homosexual tendencies," wrote in the letters page: "As a gay climber, alpinist and member of the climbing community, I find this highly offensive and immature. . . . I like to think of the climbing community as a welcoming, open-minded place, but apparently we still have a long way to go" (2010, 14). As well as some elements of the sport arguably being antigay, climbing is still also predominantly a white sport. For example, the UK's BMC, in 2006, conducted a survey of 10 percent of its 63,000 members, with a 17 percent response rate, regarding the makeup of its membership. The study revealed that though more women are now rock climbing (25% of all participants), 98 percent of people who responded to the survey were white. (This can be partially explained by the fact that white people, in general, may have more financial resources to enable them to participate or purchase equipment. Another reason may be that in some cultures there is not a history of specific ethnic groups being involved in the culture of rock climbing.) More positively, the number of respondents who classed themselves as disabled rose from 1.4 percent in 2000 to 6 percent in 2006.

Newer, individualized sports such as climbing can still position women participants as more passive than men in specific sporting contexts and construct discourses in which women are seen as less physical than men, as well as less able or less competitive, because of their biology. In an American context, Rinehart and Sydnor (2003) also state that sexism still exists in media reporting of extreme sports but, more positively, feel that in such sports categories of difference may be magnified, altered, or blurred. As a consequence, they argue political correctness can, welcomely, be thrown out.

Other aspects of identity, for example race, have also been considered in American sport. A report by Messner and colleagues (1999) found that white males dominate in the area of sports commentary. The report found that though there were few openly racist comments or images, sports programs sometimes reinforced racial stereotypes and also called attention to race or ethnicity when commenting. As well, people of color were found not to play dominant roles in sports programming commercials. These points can be seen as applicable to rock climbing. Erickson (2005) has looked at whiteness and its construction in relation to climbing from a psychoanalytic perspective, where whiteness is seen as promising a sense of "wholeness" to a climbing identity. However, in certain contexts where climbers are in stressful situations, for instance, with his example of the four U.S. climbers on a North Face expedition in Kyrgyzstan who were taken hostage in 2000, whiteness may not provide the security expected. The U.S. academic and climber Bayers (2003), in a different historical context, discusses mountaineering, imperialism, and white masculine anxieties. He argues that in the early 1900s, U.S. and English adventurers assumed a national sense of identity and purpose by assuming a racial and cultural superiority over, for instance "the 'savagery' of natives" (2). Of these differences, however, gender has received the most theoretical attention in relation to new sports such as climbing.

gender

> First woman to climb 5.14, first free ascents everywhere, champion of the world—yet all of Lynn Hill's accomplishments pale before her one-day free ascent of The Nose, an astonishing feat of skill and endurance. . . . On September 20th, 1994, Lynn Hill was the greatest rock climber in the world. (*Rock and Ice*, 1999, 78)

There is an established tradition, at least for some sections of the climbing community, of being passionately interested in issues of gender and other inequalities. The previously mentioned U.S. report (Messner et al., 1999) on boys and men in sports media, specifically in relation to the programming of extreme sports, found that commercials would often use storylines that "emphasize speed, danger, or aggressive behavior to attract viewers to their products" (10). The report concluded that, to varying degrees in the context of National Football League (NFL) games, National Basketball Association (NBA) games, Major League Baseball (MLB) games, and also extreme sports, the sports programming that boys consume shows that "a real man is strong, tough, aggressive, and above all, a winner in what is still a man's world. To be a winner he must be willing to compromise his own long-term health. . . . He must avoid being soft . . ." (11). However, though there is a growing body of work on men and masculinity in relation to extreme sport (see, for example, Robinson [2008] on climbing, Wheaton [2000] on windsurfing, Thorpe [2010] on snowboarding, and Borden [2001] on skateboarding), more work to date has been done that has focused on female sporting participants.

An article published on the biggest UK climbing forum looked at climbing's history in the 1970s and early 1980s and concluded that, in this period, mixed teams at the crag were a rarity and that if a woman was climbing, she was more often than not being "taken" climbing by a boy-friend (Ryan, 2005). The American climber Laura Waterman confirms this when she references climbing in a past era:

> Back around twenty, twenty-five years ago when I started climbing no women were leading hard climbs. None that I heard about anyway. I know for sure that no women back then were leading at the top of the day's standard. Certainly not at the Gunks, which is where I learned to climb. . . . As for ice, I had never heard of a woman in the Northeast leading ice at all. Very, very few even followed it. On many occasions Guy and I went to Chapel Pond and Huntington Ravine, and I can scarcely ever recall another woman going to the top of the Big Slab or staying at the Harvard Cabin. Lonely times. (Waterman and Waterman, 1993, 291)

However, things have moved on from the "lone climbing woman," such that women are increasingly climbing with a variety of partners, including other women. The U.S. climber Kaydee Summers (pers. comm.) describes how a group of women in the Salt Lake City, Utah, area are not letting motherhood impede their climbing progress as they take their children to sport climb with them. Women are also being regularly featured in the climbing media for their achievements, and the top female climbers are sending the hardest routes alongside the elite male climbers. For example, in 2010, after a summer of multiple Bouldering World Cup wins and podium finishes, Anna Stohr was only the second woman in the world to send a confirmed V13: "Riverbed" in Magic Wood, Switzerland (Fox, 2010, para. 1).

Historically, in the United Kingdom, notable achievements by female climbers have been made in the past by Fliss Butler (first E6 on-sight), Rachel Farmer (first F8a), Glenda Huxter (first E7 on-sight), Ruth Jenkins (first F8b), Lucy Creamer (E7 and F8a on-sights, F8b+ redpoint), Airlie Anderson (first E7), and Clare Murphy (first Font 8a+) (McClure, 2009). In Canada, women are also achieving climbing successes. Canadian climber Ellen Powick, for example, works full time as an information technology security engineer in Salt Lake City, but she also has over ninety-five 5.13 redpoints under her belt. At Maple Canyon in Utah, she has climbed "Pipedream" (5.14a), and she may be the first Canadian woman to have climbed this grade (Raleigh, 2010b). Further, in a climbing magazine article in 2011, Katherine Smith details a number of inspirational Canadian female climbers in their 40s and 50s who are still climbing hard and demonstrating commitment, passion, and energy, including Terri Frank, aged 43, Jan Ito, 44, and Karen McGilvray, 50 (Smith, 2011).

In addition, websites exist such as *Chicks Climbing* (http://www.chickswithpicks.net/), which hosts *Chicks with Picks* and *Chicks Rock*. These sites were founded to support and encourage female climbers in the United States by providing "rock clinics" where beginners and more advanced climbers can learn new ice- and rock-climbing skills. But, as detailed above, this state of affairs has not always been the case, and, some would argue, there are still not enough women climbing at the hardest grades. Others go further and state that women are still discriminated against in the sport of rock climbing. In climbing, for instance, the term "belay bunnies" continues to be used for women who don't usually climb but who hold the ropes of their male partners to ensure that they can climb safely (Robinson, 2008). Other derogative terms used include "belay bitch" or "belay slave."

Feminist sport scholars have theorized women's exclusion from mainstream sport, and the prejudice they face from men in diverse sporting contexts, in a number of ways, emphasising power relationships in the process. Some of these studies have been on gender and rock climbing (see, for example, Dilley, 2007; Plate, 2007; and Summers, 2007). For instance, there have been challenges to the idea that rock climbing as a sport is necessarily masculine and one in which femininity and athleticism are seen as contradictory. Further, research shows that traditional views on gender and biology can be questioned: "What can be inferred from men using traditionally feminine characteristics such as grace and balance to show strength and courage, while women utilise their femininity to engage in 'risky' masculine behaviours?" (Plate, 2007, 3). Assumptions that equate strength just with male sportsmen and the attributes of balance and grace solely with women are becoming increasingly challenged the more women climbers achieve the same as men and enter the elite levels of the sport. Such shifts can enable traditional masculine behavior and practices to be challenged.

Research with Australian climbers found that both sexes have accepted stereotypical assumptions regarding gender (Kiewa, 2001). In this study, both male and female participants believed that women tend to focus more on climbing relationships while men concentrate more on the activity itself. In reality, however, individual climbers were seen to support, or indeed resist, such assumptions.

The research also found that although there were variations in how individual female and male climbers conformed to gender expectations in practice, there was little deviation from gendered *expectations* as such. For instance, in her study, Kiewa (2001) found one male climber who felt he could be more open and forceful in his opinions when climbing with men rather than women, with whom, he said, you had to "step round things" (Kiewa, 2001, 9). Indeed, some women climbers themselves believe that biological differences exist between the sexes so that men are better able to climb more strenuous routes, for example overhangs on climbs that require a lot of strength.

Yet male and female rock climbers can also be seen to have diverse, and sometimes contradictory, attitudes to the increasing numbers of women climbers, thus illustrating the importance of taking care not to polarize the experiences of climbers of both sexes.

risk

In recent times, the concept of risk has become an important issue in the social sciences. As high-risk extreme sports have grown in popularity, however, there is still a lack of empirical work on the meanings people give to *voluntary* risk taking, which a sport such as climbing can be seen to illustrate (however, see Laurendeau [2006] on this issue in relation to skydiving). Tulloch and Lupton (2003) illustrate this with the example of people taking part in activities that society in general perceives as risky, but the participants themselves do not, as some of the climbers I discuss below demonstrate. (There have been calls to ban climbing since its inception, most famously from Queen Victoria in Britain, following the Matterhorn disaster of 1865.)

Research on Australian surfers has revealed that voluntary risk taking is done for many different reasons. These range from the need for thrills and excitement, to overcoming personal fears and exercising personal agency, as well as for emotional engagement, control, and self-improvement (Stranger, 1999). All these reasons could apply to the sport of climbing.

What are the biological arguments that can help explain an individual's risk-taking behaviour and a need for thrills in an extreme sport such as rock climbing? For instance, experiencing fear and pain or pleasure in a sporting activity can provoke the body to have a chemical reaction. This can lead to increased adrenaline and endorphin levels and thus influence the decision made to continue to "risk it" or not. Endorphins are chemicals in the brain known as neurotransmitters, and these transmit electrical signals in the nervous system. At least 20 different types have been identified in humans. Stress and pain cause such chemicals to be released in to the body. Endorphins cause euphoria as well as minimize any stress and pain that are experienced, due to participating in extreme sports, for example (Stoppler and Shiel, 2007).

Such chemical factors can be seen to influence whether a hard move on a route is attempted or abandoned, whether there is an attempt at the summit, or whether the climber in question takes a rest and carefully assesses the options for continuing. Bodily changes, such as the effects of high-altitude climbing, can also dramatically affect the individual's energy levels. Moreover, retardation of both thought and action can occur through high-altitude climbing, which can then affect as well as produce complex internal responses such as a loss of focus or will to continue with the climb (Bahrke and Shukitt-Hale,1993).

As well as taking chemical changes in the body into account, how does individual psychology affect risk-taking behavior, or even predispose someone to take up a risky activity such as climbing in the first place? As early as the 1960s, research was being conducted that explored the diverse motivations people had to indulge in risk-taking behaviour, how people made cognitive judgements to risk taking based on intelligence levels, how individuals reacted differently to the consequences of their risk-taking behaviours, and how important personality was in causing people to take risk or to be more conservative (Kogan and Wallach, 1964). More recently, this research has been applied to a range of risk and extreme sports such as snowboarding (Anna, Jan, and Aleksander, 2007), BASE jumping (Griffith et al., 2006), and high-altitude climbing (Fave, Bassi, and Massimini, 2003).

Zuckerman and Kuhlman (2000) linked different types of risk-taking behavior such as drinking, sex, and drug taking to the personality of 260 college students using a personality test questionnaire. Generalized risk taking was then related to scales on aspects such as impulsive sensation seeking, aggression, and sociability; gender differences were also considered. In addition, biological traits associated with both risk taking and personality were considered to be important. These factors included the

enzyme monoamine oxidase, the D4 dopamine receptor gene, and aug-
mentation or reduction of the cortical evoked potential. Zuckerman
(2000) defines *sensation seeking* as a willingness to take part in activities
such as extreme sports, for example, rock climbing, and concluded that
risk taking is not the main point for these sensation seekers. Instead, he
concluded that this is the price that people are willing to pay for having
their need for change and excitement satisfied. Further, he found that risk
takers are not necessarily anxious or neurotic personality types. He also
linked genetic variance in risk-taking behavior, such as participating in
extreme sports, to genetics. Young men are seen to have greater levels
of the sex hormone testosterone than women do. This can be seen to
account for young men's risk-taking activities being at their highest in
adolescence. Though women have less testosterone, this hormone is
linked by him to those women whose behavior is similar to men's, such
as showing aggression and being assertive.

However, evidence from extreme-sports participants complicates these
biological explanations for risk-taking behavior. Rock climbers in the
United Kingdom that I interviewed took offense at often being labeled
by the media as "out of control" thrill seekers, who had no option but to
pursue such activities due to genetics or being a particular personality
type. One man, in his 40s, keen to show he considered risk taking very
carefully, said, "It must be safer climbing on big walls when you know
what you're doing, than walking down a street in London—so it's a
balance of risk, you know?" (cited in Robinson, 2008, 150).

In the context of mountaineering, sports psychologists Fave, Bassi, and
Massimini (2003) argue that risk actually plays a minor role in climbing,
if seen in line with a goal-directed approach to risk seeking. They also
found that the opportunity for experiencing "flow" may help motivate
climbers to take part in a risky expedition Thus, they conclude that studies
on motivation in extreme sports need to distinguish between risk and
searching for challenges or opportunities for action.

Yet it is not in dispute that climbers get injured. An article on rock-
climbing-induced injuries found that three-quarters of elite and recreational sport climbers suffered from upper extremity injuries. Around
60 percent of these injuries involve both the hand and wrist, while the
other 40 percent are divided equally between the elbow and the shoulder
(Rooks, 1997). (See also Chapter 3, "Science.")

A risk sport such as climbing and other such activities have also been
described by the term "edgework" (Lyng, 2005). Originally developed

by social scientist Stephen Lyng, this more sociological way of examining risk behaviour takes into account social factors in exploring risk taking:

> What draws people to "extreme sports," dangerous occupations, and other edgework activities is the intensely seductive character of the experience itself. As the participants themselves report, they do it because "it's fun!" The challenge—to explain *how* life-threatening experiences come to acquire a seductively appealing character in the contemporary social context—requires a complex sociological theory of structure and agency in late modernity. (Lyng, 2005, 5)

In this theory, risk-taking experiences are best understood as undertaken to escape diverse aspects of contemporary life, including institutionalized routines.

Rock climbers can also be seen, at one level, to be courting the academic Lash's (1993, 2000) "terrible sublime" of death by engaging in the risky sporting practices that climbing entails. The U.S. climbing journalist Bisharat states:

> Life is an uphill road, punctuated by many happy milestones—moments that make the trip seem worth taking. There are the inevitable, profuse potholes, too—and the deeper ones may make you consider abandoning the ride all together. But if everything were easy, it wouldn't be "fun"—advice I routinely impart to wobbling sport climbers, cussing themselves and dangling at the ends of their ropes, their sinewy little limbs punching the air in comical frustration. If you're not willing to fail, you'll never succeed, especially in climbing. (2010a, para. 1)

However, with technical and technological developments, traditional climbing can be made so much safer nowadays, with the risks, to some extent at least, minimized. Rock climbers can climb much harder routes than in the past when safety was more of an issue.

The UK climber Simon Yates (2002) argues that, in his experience of working as a roped access worker (that is, someone who uses his or her rope skills, often gained through rock climbing or other sports, to earn a living), the safest workers were those who were also climbers and cavers. In his opinion, this is because workers had rope skills to protect themselves and could assess danger as well as rationalize fear. They were also unafraid of heights in the course of their work and were cool under pressure, while other workers on roped access sites were either not aware of the dangers or stupidly and actively courted risk.

Yet it could be argued that the climbers Yates refers to do not take risks in their working environment because their livelihood depends on their safety. However, in the actual everyday practices of rock climbing, they may be more likely not to be rational or safety conscious, given that risk for *some* climbers may be the point, and not just a side effect, of the activity. As opposed to the climber I cited above who said he did not take unnecessary risks, and in opposition to Zuckerman's views cited previously, the view that risk is *actively* sought by climbers and other extreme-sports enthusiasts is held by other theorists who are concerned with analyzing people's behavior across a range of risk activities. For example, Smith (2005) discusses financial trading as a high-risk activity, comparing this to risk sports, which are conceptualized as those where the people involved in them maximize, rather than minimize, risk activity. He argues, "Most skydivers. . . . and other leisure risk takers fervently embrace the risk factors of their sport" (Smith, 2005, 188).

Do climbers take needless risks? The following account by a journalist of climbing in Yosemite in the early 1980s could be taken as evidence that they do:

> I just tied a few gallons of water to the bottom of the haul bag and hoped it would do. As I reached under the haul bag to slake my thirst from one of those bottles, I blanched to find that both jugs had sprung leaks and were nearly empty. With nearly 2,000 feet of stone still overhead, I contemplated the wisdom of forging on, then grabbed the rack and set off determined to go fast. (Raleigh, 2010a, para. 7)

More evidence of risk taking can be seen by looking at male mountaineers, and the view that some of them often savor life's pleasures to the full after they return from a risky mountaineering trip, as the danger involved has made them appreciate being alive (Coffey, 2003). To further support this connection between climbing and danger, many climbers know another rock climber or a mountaineer who has died or been seriously injured.

The UK academic and climber Terry Gifford (2004) problematizes the distinction between risky and nonrisky activities when he states that a climber does not necessarily need to be a highly technical or elite climber to have to deal with the possibility of death. For him, "if there's no risk, there's no climbing" (9). It is not, therefore, only the elite climbers who face dangerous situations when climbing. All climbers can find themselves unexpectedly in an "extreme" environment. Sometimes, however, this extreme situation can come from the most unpredictable quarters. This is something a male climber from the United States found when he ventured to Lizard Lake, Marble, Colorado, to check out some south-facing cliffs that seemed to offer both easy access and all-day sun necessary for cragging in the mountains in winter time. To his surprise, he was almost shot at by a "hillbilly," who clearly saw climbers as sport during the deer hunting season (Jackson, 2010b)!

Of relevance here is the idea of edgework mentioned previously. Also relevant is Gifford's (2006) argument that "Testing the edge of control is what climbing is about. ... Between control and risk is the field of personal action, a matter of degrees of judgement for each climber based upon ability, experience, the conditions, her judgement of him and his judgment of her" (160). This includes decisions made about the safety of a climb and the weather conditions, whether a route is within the limits of the technical skills and experience of a particular climber, and so on. However, an individual's assessment of the risk involved can go beyond the act of climbing itself, as the example above illustrates.

Also, there is a random element involved in risk taking in climbing (many accidents in rock climbing, for example, take place not on the climb itself but from descending down the cliff afterwards). And even climbing indoors in a gym is not without attendant risks. A report in the journal *Wilderness and Environmental Medicine* compiled rates and types of injury occurring in the 2005 Indoor World Championships in Munich. This involved 500 climbers from 55 countries and found that the injury rate was 3.1 per 1,000 hours of climbing, compared to national football, which was at a rate of 30.3 per 1,000 hours. They concluded, therefore, that indoor rock climbing "has a low injury risk and a very good safety profile in high-level competition" (cited in *Climb and More.com*, 2007, 14). But others argue differently.

As a comparison, in a UK context, there are deaths at climbing walls connected to a failure to tie in or to do up a harness safely, or from belayers' errors (Codling, 1998). So, even when taking care to minimize risks, the consequences are still arbitrarily experienced (Yates, 2002). Yet risk taking can also be educative in the opinion of some climbers: "First time you get injured. You learn a lot when you're unable to climb. This is an important

Rescue workers begin the treacherous ascent with a litter carrying an injured climber in the mountains near Evergreen, Colorado. The all-volunteer group from Alpine Rescue is on call around the clock. Each summer many inexperienced climbers are seriously injured in the Colorado mountains. (AP/Wide World Photos)

experience that just plain sucks. But you don't have to be moving to make progress. Everyone should learn to be still" (Bisharat, 2010a, para. 12).

However, such decisions taken about the level of risk involved, or that has to be controlled, have an ethical context. This can be seen when individual climbers decide not to bolt certain types of rock, such as gritstone in the United Kingdom, due to local, regional, and national ethics that forbid this, or decide to establish sport climbs that have a lesser degree of difficulty and risk than trad climbing. For example, in the United States, sport climbing did not apparently have an easy birth. There were fights in Yosemite's Camp 4 parking lot in the 1980s between Mark Chapman and John Bachar because of how bolts were being placed. If you favored bolting, there was a risk that the tires on your truck might be slashed by antibolt traditionalists. This could be seen as a clash between those in Europe, many of whom were in support of bolting, and the conservative trad climbers from the United States who refused to bolt (Ryan, 2008).

To go against such tradition entails, at different historical times, risking the disapproval of the climbing community, sometimes, as with the example of sport climbing above, for very opposed reasons.

Examples of recent incidents involving those climbers who are antibolting, for ethical and environmental reasons, include one of the United States' most notorious bolt choppers, Ken from Nichols, Connecticut, recently apparently ceasing a 20-year career of deliberately chopping bolts from climbs after he was banned from specific crags, fined, and given probation. However, the antibolting tradition continues, with reports that he is suspected to still be chopping. Debates on climbing ethics and styles can, however, come down in the end to just personal choice. Moreover, the debates about how risky "authentic" climbing should be, and which climbing styles are in themselves authentic, remain at the heart of such different opinions.

In addition, climbers can also construct a view of themselves as being risk takers in their youth or early adulthood, then, perhaps on entering middle age, becoming more risk conscious or averse. Moreover, a consideration of risk taking in climbing can also reveal the need to consider changes over the life course in a climber's individual biography in interaction with the different kinds of everyday climbing activity undertaken. For instance, a climber from Oregon, writing about risk in the context of free soloing, says:

I have chosen not to free solo on the basis that the others in my life mean more to me than such a pursuit. How we answer these ethical questions impacts our youth. I say this because to glorify free soloing is to encourage youngsters to blatantly risk death. And that is the difference between free soloing and roped climbing. We have a responsibility as an older generation to ensure that the youth of tomorrow have a chance to understand the true meaning of freedom and adventure. (Klimt, 2010, 12)

However, others disagree with this stance: "Nobody has the right to criticize and condemn the free-soloists. To do so is to expose oneself as an envious and unimaginative dolt" (Van Middlebrook, 2010, 12).

In their discussion of extreme skiing, Kay and Laberge (2003) note that some skiers think that taking increased risks will avenge those who have already died: "It apparently gives solace to those left alive that death is noble in the name of freedom ... or a steeper descent" (392). Motivations for increased risk taking can, therefore, be seen as complex. Also, risk taking does not always have noble intentions behind it. For example, recent deaths on Everest, which, arguably, could have been avoided if those mountaineers passing others not yet dead were not so focused on summiting (Maley, 2006), show that risky pursuits, far from being either ethical or noble, can be seen to be individualistic and selfish in the extreme. As the U.S. academic and climber Vause (1997) argues, with the commitment to climb, a climber must realize there also comes responsibility and possibly death as a result of those choices.

For both male and female climbers, the social and political context of risk in society affects how they pursue, and experience, their chosen sport. This can be seen in a number of ways. Specifically, in a British context, official government reports state that it has become a risk-averse nation (Brindle and Lewis, 2006). The present risk-averse culture can eliminate the national urge to explore and seek out adventure because of more and more regulation. Conversely, Reith (1999) argues that voluntary or recreational risk taking becomes more tolerated, or even encouraged in society, as public organizations strive to make modern life safer. Yet, as Douglas (1999) notes, adventure package-tour operators do all they can to minimize risks as it is in their financial interests to do so. Douglas feels that the outdoors is not an extended leisure center, and therefore risk cannot be fully eliminated, a view agreed with by Watters (2003), who, in arguing that it is important not to let marketing, peer pressure, or bravado influence our own personal threshold of acceptable risk, states, "Once the fanfare is stripped away, these activities are real—real enough to kill people" (266).

On her website, the American superstar climber Lynn Hill discusses how she was worried about being exposed to liability because of her involvement in climbing camps. She feels that a climbing accident at one of the camps could potentially lead to her being sued, whether it was due to her negligence or not. However, she states that now, more than ever before, society needs people to engage with pursuits such as climbing that encourage us to take personal responsibility: "In the end, no matter whether we choose to take part in so-called risky activities or not, life is full of unexpected accidents and no amount of money or denial of one's own personal or moral responsibility can stop them from happening" (Hill, 2005, para. 2).

Furthermore, while there is a fear that, for example, insurance costs and child-protection legislation will stop climbing clubs taking young people out to climb, rescue teams do not want to legislate for people going out in bad weather (Douglas, 2007). These restrictions would inevitably take away an integral part of risk-taking activities. Rescue workers suggest instead that learning survival skills from older people, as part of an apprenticeship where individuals learn over a period of time, for example, what to do if the weather turns nasty or vital equipment is lost, is important. However, this passing down of outdoor skills from an older generation is a dying custom, at least to some extent. Moreover, experience cannot always offer protection. An early pioneer of sport climbing, Kurt Albert (who also invented the idea of "redpointing" after he painted a small red point at the bottom of a climb to show that it had been climbed completely free), died in 2010 from a fall on a route in Germany. Despite much experience of big-wall climbing in places such as Pakistan and Patagonia, this knowledge could not prevent his death (MacDonald, 2010).

Climbers, despite knowing the risks, still continue to climb, sometimes at the edge of or beyond their limits. As Kurt Albert himself said, in what was to be one of his last interviews, "I look for freedom, and I always question standards and rules—I like to do it my way. I don't like dogma" (Albert, cited in Guthrie, 2010, para. 5).

Again, there are gender dimensions, even in relation to risk. Arlene Blum, the American pioneering mountaineer, now in her 60s, explored being both a mother and mountaineer in her book *Breaking Trail* (Blum 2005). Here, she examines the paradox that she needed to climb for herself to be a woman but was not seen as a woman if she was also a climber, especially regarding the spectacular risk-taking mountaineering for which she was known. Conversely, Coffey (2004) discusses the views of a male mountaineer who had made a decision to take less risk in the mountain after taking on a new family: "The need for adventure, he believes, is hard-wired into some human beings, part of our natural evolution. 'That's why risk-takers have to go out on the hunt,' he said, 'but they're not hunting animals anymore, they're not providing game for the table, they're going out and proving themselves against a challenge. It goes right to the ego of men' " (Coffey, 2004, 11). In this way, it can be seen that men are admired for managing danger, especially, in the media, the elite climbers. However, women are not always accorded the same accolade.

One of the most famous examples of this tendency in recent times is the example of female mountaineer Alison Hargreaves, who died on K2 in 1998, and the subsequent media reaction to her as a mother due to placing herself at risk. When men take risks with their lives on mountains, they are seen as heroic and brave, but female adventurers are often perceived in the media as selfish, driven, and egocentric: "Where women are involved in dangerous pursuits, all sorts of cultural definitions and limitations are placed upon their behaviour" (Palmer, 2004, 65).

Another American climber, Kaydee Summers (2007), in discussing mountaineers who are also parents, notes that women and men often take the decision to place themselves in risk situations on mountains from different positions. For example, it is usually female climbers who have to think about childcare on an expedition and whether to take children to base camp, as they are most likely to be the primary caregiver. She concludes that gender inequalities are still present in the climbing community and are particularly apparent if climbers are parents, especially as mothers. However, women climbers and mountaineers can have different opinions over this issue. American mountaineer Ellen Miller was quoted recently as saying, "For me personally, and I think for many women, either you want to climb or you want to have a family. I don't think many women can do both very well" (cited in Stirling, 2009, para. 1).

Yet climbers of both sexes continue to take risks in the name of adventure, freedom, and friendship as they have done in the past, as the climber Chuck Pratt's version of the successful 1964 first ascent of the south face of Mount Watkins, Yosemite, with Chouinard and Harding attests. He recounts that although they had brought enough water for four days, it was going to be at least five days before they summited. The hot weather conditions were almost unbearable, especially without enough water supplies:

> Warren had nearly fainted several times from the heat, Yvon was speechless with fatigue, and I was curled up in a semi-stupor trying to utilize a small patch of shade beneath an overhanging boulder. . . . By the fourth day Yvon had lost so much weight from dehydration that he could lower his climbing knickers without undoing a single button. (Pratt, 2002, 57–58)

But despite such hardship, he feels that the climb was a victory and fulfilment for which all the climbers involved were forever grateful, and was the reason they continued to climb. Thus, both male and female climbers take risks not just for their own sake but for the diversity of rewards, both tangible and otherwise, that climbing affords those who are prepared to suffer and risk life and limb.

As this discussion of risk in climbing illustrates, the issues regarding climbers' social, psychological, and physiological motives to climb; the commercialization of the sport; and gender cannot be neatly separated. For example, the sex of a climber is, in some cases, connected to the reasons risks are taken and the ways such risks are perceived by others. Furthermore, the reasons people climb may be to take risks but also to control them. Climbing can be a sport undertaken for the sheer love of it but also for the material rewards newer developments such as sponsorship of climbers can bring. In this way, the increasing commercialization of the sport can be seen to detract from climbing's antiestablishment ethos, but it also allows more people to participate as numbers involved in the sport grow.

2. origins

the history of American rock climbing is about people *and* places. This includes events and happenings, significant moments in the sport's development, and different groups of climbers; all of which emerged over time in diverse areas of the United States' vast and geographically varied terrain. It is equally about the exploits of outstanding sporting men and women in various parts of the United States and the globe as well as more ordinary mortals. It is a vibrant history that is both human and natural in form, for the history cannot be told without seeing the different kinds of rock as fundamental to this colorful history.

The terrain has allowed different climbing styles and techniques to evolve over decades to the present day. This was made possible by, it is said, the risk taking, courage, and chutzpah of the climbing visionaries and leaders from the nineteenth century to the present day: "The American climber has always been a maverick, often an eccentric, at times virtually a social outcast" (Tejada-Flores, 1997, 8). Further, as Mellor (2001) puts it: "Climbing, to me, isn't just climbing. It's experiencing places and people, and it's relishing their variety" (9). Sometimes the connections between people and geographical places and events have been controversial and explosive, as this chapter details. The history of rock climbing in the United States is also about the different cultures, climbing "tribes," and lifestyles that have emerged around these diverse times and places that make up the trajectory of American rock climbing.

No short chapter can do justice to or provide a full history of American rock climbing or cover in sufficient depth the varying regions within which specific types of climbing takes place over different time frames. Furthermore, though this book highlights both past and recent achievements by climbers, the rapidly changing nature of the sport will ensure that since this book was published, some of the achievements noted here will since have been bettered. This diversity exists through Adirondack and

33

White Mountain granite, home to New England traditionalism; sport climbing in the red sandstone towers of the desert Southwest; the steep walls and
overhanging sandstone in the Southeast; the Shawangunks, the terrain of
the infamous Vulgarians; Utah's canyons; Western big-wall climbing on
the white walls of Sierra granite; and high-altitude mountaineering in the
Rockies, Tetons, and Cascades (Mellor, 2001).

Areas such as Red River Gorge, Kentucky; Smith Rock, Oregon;
Hueco Tanks, Texas; and the Moab area, Utah, could be contenders for
contemporary climbing hot spots and are referred to later in Chapter 4,
"Places and Events." In this chapter, however, I trace the historical origins
of and developments in American rock climbing in relation to three central areas: the Shawangunks, Yosemite, and Colorado. These three areas
serve as case studies that have historically been at the forefront of stylistic,
technical, and cultural developments in U.S. climbing.

beginnings

The historical routes of rock climbing in the United States can be traced
back to alpinism and mountaineering. The climbing writer Mazel (1991)
argues that a specific American mountaineering tradition did exist even
before the late 1800s, if one defines a mountaineer as "anyone who climbs
up a mountain, regardless of the difficulty of the feat or the motivations
underlying it" (5). This is seen as a different view to one that views mountaineering as a sport carried out purely for its own sake, which constitutes
a challenge and entails some level of technical difficulty. In this case, the
sport can be seen as starting later. Mazel outlines the sport after the birth
of alpinism, commonly dated at 1786, when Mont Blanc was first
ascended. European climbers also took to other ascents with great enthusiasm, but not so in the United States. In fact, it was not until social changes
occurred so that Americans had both leisure time and the finances for
mountaineering that the early twentieth century saw mountain clubs
spring up in places such as San Francisco, New York, Boston, Denver,
and Seattle. Further, because of the U.S. emphasis on the importance of
wilderness, exploration, and mapping the land, a number of early ascents
were made by surveyors. In this context, climbing for its own sake made
much less sense (see Chapter 3, "Science").

Where and how did mountaineering evolve into rock climbing?
Certainly, this was a process rather than something that can be encapsu-
lated by a single event, but certain events do stand out. Climbing author

Chris Jones (1997) describes how, in 1916, 28-year-old professor Albert Ellingwood, from Colorado College, bucked the trend of seeing the area's 50-plus summits (counting those in excess of 14,000 feet) merely as a reason to undertake a "strenuous hike." Thus, in appreciating a hard rock climb merely for its own sake, he and fellow climbers made three successful first ascents in the Sangre de Cristo Range, very occasionally using a rope to do so. These were, Jones argues, most likely the first U.S. rock climbs where there was a conscious effort to belay.

The American climber and writer Pat Ament (2002b) gives a different spin to events. He asserts that Native Americans were, in all probability, the first human climbers on this continent. He gives as examples the Arapaho and Ute who took to the rocks of Boulder, Colorado, while Apaches are linked to the granite of Prescott, Arizona. The reasons they did this, he argues, were to gain positions of advantage over their enemies or to be able to transmit messages. For Ament (2002b), gender is also important to mention in the early history of American rock climbing:

> Those who ventured onto the steepest walls of Colorado's Flatirons in the early 1900s didn't have to do any deep thinking to realize the potential of the great rocks which rise so prominently above the city of Boulder. Some of these climbers were women—wearing long dresses, wide hats, and shiny, large-heeled shoes—who found themselves flush against the stone and crawling upward. (1)

In fact, before the 1960s, rock climbing was generally seen as the "poor cousin" of mountaineering because the United States mostly was not suitable for "proper alpinism" (Achey, Chelton, & Godfrey, 2001, 28). Further, the authors say, it was not until the 1960s that a culture of rock climbing was established that was virtually independent of mountaineering. This was when climbing started to be a way of life for some of the most infamous characters associated with the sport, and not just a part-time leisure pursuit.

How then did rock climbing in the United States develop from such beginnings into the multifaceted sport it is today, including the shift from aid to free climbing and the establishment of sport climbing, bouldering, indoor climbing, and competition climbing, for instance? To answer this question, even though the kind and prevalence of different climbing activities at these areas has ebbed and flowed over the years, we must look to the great climbing areas of the Shawangunks, Yosemite, and Colorado.

the "gunks"

In the book *Yankee Rock and Ice: A History of Climbing in the North Eastern United States* (1993), Laura and Guy Waterman define this area as encompassing New England plus eastern New York (which is further identified as the Catskills, Hudson Highlands, Adirondacks, and Shawangunks). In the Northeast area, most of the climbing can be split into rock climbing in warm weather or ice climbing in winter, for example, on Mount Washington. The Watermans report that there are recorded instances of early ice climbs taking place on the glacial cirques of Mount Washington, for example, at the start of the twentieth century.

But it is the Shawangunks which are the focus here, given their importance to rock climbing history. The rock in the area is dense quartzite, which is harder than granite. Situated around 90 miles north of Manhattan, the mountains are pronounced "Shon-gums" but are known simply as the Gunks, and they are the mecca of Eastern U.S. rock climbing: "The Gunks are to eastern climbers what Pipeline is to surfers (in Hawaii), what Fifth Ave. is to models (in New York City), what Beale Street is to blues men (in Memphis, Tennessee). In other words: world class" (Fallesen, 2011, para. 1).

Furthermore, more people make the trip to the Gunks on the weekend than to other U.S. climbing hot spots such as Hueco Tanks, Texas; Yosemite, California; or Eldorado Canyon, Colorado. (Much of the northern ridge in the area is protected and held as the Mohonk Preserve, Minnewaska State Park Preserve, and Sam's Point Preserve. Here there are more than 100 miles of both hiking trails and different climbing areas.) Further, it could be argued that no other world-class climbing area can equal the moderate grades, 5.5 to 5.7, to be found in abundance at the Gunks: "There you find elegant lines, intricate moves, delicate traverses, strenuous verticality, intimidating roofs, and breathtaking exposure" (Schwartz, 1993, 101). And so the 1960s through 1980s saw some of the best climbers in the world come to test their climbing mettle on the quartz cliffs of The Trapps, Near Trapps, Millbrook, and Sky Top.

The Gunks' history can be traced from the 1930s. Fritz Wiessner, a mountaineer and immigrant from Germany, was the first to climb there. His first ascent was "Old Route," at Millbrook, which is both the most remote and tallest cliff at the Gunks. He then quickly established a number of what were to be classic routes, including "Skytop." Wiessner, along with Hans Kraus, continued to spend his climbing energies on putting up routes at The Trapps and Near Trapps, which are the two main crags in the area (Bronski, 1996). The route "High Exposure," first climbed by the pair in 1941, has been seen by some to be the best single rock-climbing route in the world: "Because of this awesome reputation, and its incredible photogenic character, this classic usually makes its way onto almost every list of 'must-do' routes for visiting climbers" (Bronski 1996, para. 3).

The Shawangunks held the position of center stage in the Northeast U.S. climbing culture during the late 1950s and mid 1960s. According to Waterman and Waterman (1993), standards of difficult climbing here increased rapidly during this period, in both technical terms and "in establishing a code of free-climbing ethics, style, and environmental concern" (171–72). This made the Shawangunks an appealing site for those seeking more challenging climbs. At this time, James P. McCarthy was widely viewed as the most prominent climber in the area. But in 1961, his chief rival, Dick Williams, "bagged" the second ascent of Chouinard's *Matinee*, when even McCarthy had not done that route's first pitch.

The ethical and stylistic standards were also of paramount importance during this period. As Waterman and Waterman (1993) explain, "not only was it unacceptable to pull upon a piton or sling, but most leaders felt it was equally inexcusable to rest even temporarily by artificial means" (179). In other words, equipment such as carabiners, pitons, and ropes were only deemed appropriate if a climber fell; they were not to be used for resting or assisting the climber on their ascent. Moreover, it has been seen that the pure style and ethics of the Gunks foreshadowed later debates in the 1980s on climbing ethics in relation to sport as opposed to more traditional climbing styles. Other key names of the 1960s and 1970s who advanced climbing standards in this region were John Stannard, Steve Wunsch, John Bragg, and Henry Barber, opening the grades up from 5.10 to 5.11 and beyond.

In the 1980s, due to increased climbing standards and technological advancements in climbing gear, many difficult new climbs were established and the Gunks became a world-class climbing area. For instance, the female rock-climbing legend Lynn Hill, in 1984 at the Gunks, performed an on-sight (climbing with no prior knowledge or practice) first ascent of "Yellow Crack," 5.12R/X: "In her book, *Climbing Free*, Hill said that she learned that climbing in the Gunks was 'as difficult as it was exhilarating'" (Fallesen, 2011, para. 7). Other female climbers achieving hard grades here and in other parts of the region during the 1980s included Barbara Devine, Alison Osius, and Rosie Andrews.

However, in 1988 the Mohonk Preserve banned the use of bolts and pitons. Furthermore, the chipping or gluing of holds was also forbidden.

This has preserved the area as a traditional climbing stronghold. But one poster on a climbing forum had a different view on the legacy of the bolting ban: "Kinda similar to the bolting ban that has kept the Gunks in the backwater of modern difficulty and route development" (MarcC, 2009, para. 1).

In 1993, the climber Susan Schwartz wrote that the "elegant" area Skytop was visible from the New York State Thruway. Further, the surrounding countryside and the presence of one of the Hudson Valley's grand hotels, the Mohonk Mountain House, harked back to another era. This was one where gentlemen were expected to wear jackets when dining and afternoon tea was served. Most climbers, however, stayed at the free Appalachian Mountain Club (AMC) campground, known locally as Camp Slime.

The climbing, however, made up for such a need to "slum it" given the area's rich climbing. After successfully completing a route there, Schwartz recalls an encounter with a well-heeled guest at the Mohonk: " 'Oh, look, dear, it's a rock climber,' one immaculately groomed woman said, when I emerged sweaty and grimy from Greyface on a steamy summer afternoon. She looked so delighted, I thought maybe she'd invite me to tea" (1993, 102). It was also in the 1990s that the Gunks took off as an important bouldering area. However, climbing is currently banned at Skytop due to the area being on private land and owned by the Mohonk Mountain House.

As this example shows, the Gunks have a rich history of climbing mavericks and those who do not see themselves as part of any climbing establishment. During the late 1950s and early 1960s, the "Vulgarians" were a particularly infamous group of climbers in this area.

According to climbing writer Fox Rogers (1993), the Vulgarians emerged with the intent to mount a challenge to the "Appies," the established and more traditional, conservative AMC climbers. The original group consisted of a small number of New York City residents associated with the City College of New York outing club. But by the end of the 1960s this group had expanded to more than 40 members from different avenues of life, not all of whom were climbers. In 1958, the Appies made a move to assert more control of the climbing in the region. With the support of the Mohonk Trust (the organization that manages the land where the Gunks are situated), they established a permit system where prospective climbers needed to qualify as leaders or seconds, with the Appies judging who was to be awarded such a qualification. Understandably, this caused further tension between the Vulgarians and the Appies. As Fox

Rodgers writes, "climbing cannot be controlled. The Vulgarians took it one step further: out of control" (1993, 112).

Certainly, the Vulgarians caused extreme reactions, and people tended either to revere them or be appalled by their actions and what they symbolized with their antiestablishment stance. Adopting a certain dress code in what Jones describes as a "Brando-Kerouac" image (1997, 270), they wore Levi's, t-shirts, and, unusually for the time, imported French down jackets as well as a distinctive type of cap, the "Turswiry" hat. Jones reports a conversation between Gran, the unofficial spokesman for Eastern climbing, and the famous climber Royal Robbins, regarding just who were the "official hard men" in their respective areas. Gran reported that "in the Gunks you can tell the best climbers by the hats they wear." It sounded absurd, but it was true. The ever-earnest Robbins was taken aback and impressively replied, "In Yosemite you can tell the best climbers by the routes they do" (Jones, 1997, 271).

> **The Vulgarians' antics were detailed in the self-produced magazine, the _Vulgarian Digest_, in which sheep, women, and alcohol figured prominently. For example, the magazine reported on an incident in which the Vulgarians showered the Appies with urine after an evening of dining. They were also known for rolling over cars and, of course, the naked climbing for which they became infamous (Fox Rogers, 1993).**

Moreover, some climbers lament the fact that the kind of attitude and spirit shown by the Vulgarians no longer exists. However, John Stannard (cited in Fox Rogers, 1993), a climber at the same time, considered them a rather inferior and paler copy of the group Rock and Ice, associated with Don Whillans and Joe Brown in Britain. And in 1993, some climbers were saying that climbing at the Gunks has now more in common with the Appies than the notorious Vulgarians.

The area's historical importance for today's climbers was illustrated by the U.S. _Rock and Ice_ climbing magazine in 2009, when it published the award-winning filmmaker Josh Lowell's account "Bouldering in the Big Apple and Beyond." This was written originally in 1999 to accompany his first video on the fast-paced development of modern bouldering in that area. The region is currently known for its bouldering sites and spreads out to diverse areas in the woods around New Paltz. It has been compared to the famous bouldering region at Fontainbleau, near Paris: "There's no

Image from 1970 copy of the *Vulgarian Digest*, written for a group of climbers frequenting the Shawangunks north of New York City. (*Vulgarian Digest*)

single mega area, no experience of arriving at a motherlode of blocks like you do at, for example, the Buttermilks or Hueco Tanks. But, thanks to today's generation of active and motivated boulderers—people like Andy Salo, Andrew Zalewski, Tim Keenan, Paul Jung, Brett Lowell, Ivan Greene and many others—dozens of new areas have been found in the forests surrounding New Paltz" (Bisharat, 2010b, para. 2). Indeed, countless new areas have been found here in the last year alone, when more than 500 new "problems" were done, and it is further estimated that there are over 2,000 brand-new problems in total.

Although the earlier heyday of the Gunks is over, we cannot dismiss their prominence in the United States or wider afield. The climber Clune (2010) sings the praises of the area for being the Eastern birthplace of the 5.10 grade: "I don't care if you can dawdle on 5.13a's at the Red River gorge for 45 minutes, or if you've got that 28-move 5.12c blue route at the gym wired. A Gunks' 5.10 will give you pause" (para. 2). Further, though it may be the case that by the late 1980s the best Gunks climbs had been done, there now exist climbers such as Andy Salo and Brian Kim who are currently putting up new routes in places one would not expect (Donoso, 2011).

yosemite

Many have argued that Yosemite Valley, with its granite rock, is the beating heart of climbing in the United States. It has also been seen as possibly the most famous rock-climbing area in the world: "Yosemite Valley is a rock-climber's Mecca. The weather is good and the rock is plentiful; there are dozens of sheer faces over 1000ft. high, some reaching to three times that height. Smaller outcrops are everywhere" (Meyers, 1979, 15).

The area's importance in the history of U.S. and world climbing in terms of developments in the sport cannot be underestimated. If the 1960s can be seen as synonymous with big-wall climbing, then the 1970s are equally associated with free climbing. Alex Huber and Hainz Zak (2003), both extremely experienced at climbing in Yosemite, outline that hard free climbing (and the appearance of the cordless drill in the 1980s) in time led some climbers to adopt sport climbing. And Yosemite was a place where tensions between these different styles of climbing were infamous, as well as being known for developments in the historical shift from aid to free climbing.

The wider area of Yosemite itself is vast and includes the fantastic Needles, south near Bakersfield; the Sierra crest past its highest peaks; on past Yosemite to the blue waters and white rock of Lake Tahoe; and all the way to Castle Crags, which is in the shadow of Mount Shasta. This is where the Sierra granite goes under the more recent volcanic flows of the Cascades (Mellor, 2001). Yosemite itself divides into the Valley which comprises vast, popular walls for climbing, and Tuolumne Meadows, with its high forests and tall domes.

Climbing's early roots in the Yosemite region can be traced back to 1869 with John Muir's climbing of Cathedral Peak in the High Sierra: "It might be said that free climbing in America began as a small, obscure burst of light. Alone and enjoying the beauty of the Sierra Nevada, the 31 year old Muir simply hiked to the base of the rock and made the ascent. Muir used no rope or hardware, and no special climbing shoes" (Ament, 2002b, 7).

In the 1930s, early rock climbing in the Sierras can be characterized by the efforts of Robert Underhill and a select group of mountaineers who made an ambitious ascent of the longest and steepest face of Mount Whitney. The climbing author Jones (1997) points out that the significance of this climb was not its level of difficulty (for example, in comparison to the climbs that had previously been done in Canada or the Tetons). Rather, it was the symbolism inherent in the fact that the most impressive face on what was the Sierras' highest peak had been conquered. From this event it could be said that what we know as modern rock climbing developed.

In the area, Tahquitz Rock also had one of the most important roles in rock climbing from the 1930s onwards. In fact, Tahquitz climbers invented the rating system that contemporary climbers use (Mellor,

Naturalist and author John Muir, ca. 1902. As a champion of preserving the beauty of California's Yosemite Valley, Muir was a dominant figure in the conservation movement of the late 19th and early 20th centuries. (Library of Congress)

Legendary climber Warren Harding on the first ascent of the Wall of the Early Morning Light, a 27-day epic on sheer cliffs and overhangs in Yosemite National Park, California. (AP/Wide World Photos)

2001). Moreover, after the mid-1940s, due to World War II and the lack of transportation and funds, climbing in more local areas, such as the San Francisco Bay area, became the norm. Climbers had little money, so had to make do with ex-army equipment and clothes, such as Vibram-soled army boots, which cost $5, and tennis sneakers.

As well as noting these trends in climbing gear, Jones (1997) points out that climbers of the day, including Robin Hansen, Fritz Lippmann, John Salathé, and Ax Nelson, were interested in climbing classic routes such as the southwest face of Half Dome, the Lost Arrow Chimney, and the north face of Sentinel. To conquer the problems inherent in climbing very smooth and steep granite cliffs, breakthroughs in the fashioning of pitons by Salathé and the use of nylon ropes after World War II allowed Salathé and Nelson to climb Lost Arrow, if with some hardship. This was a significant event in the history of North American climbing. Salathé recalled about the event "V ver pooped out till ve thought ve ver dead" (cited in Jones, 1997, 180).

Even still, in the mid 1950s, Yosemite climbing in the main was inexpert. Characters such as Warren Harding and Mark Powell, unlike many others of the day, gave up college to climb full time: "This was a major break with the past. It marked the change from the career man who climbed on weekends to the climber who supported his habit as best he could" (Jones, 1997, 194). And thus the "climbing bum" was born.

In 1957, the climber Robbins, with Michael Sherrick and Jerry Gallwas, took five days to summit the northwest face of Half Dome, beating Harding's team. It was, at the time, the most demanding big-wall climb in the country and the first Grade VI on the continent. However, in 1957, Harding, Powell, and Bill "Dolt" Feuerer conquered El Capitan. This was the very sheer 2,900-foot face, which had not been climbed due to techniques not being advanced enough at the time. (In addition, it was 900 feet higher than the northwest face of Half Dome.) Harding said, reflecting on the climb, "However, as I hammered in the last bolt, and staggered over the rim, it was not clear to me who was conqueror and who was conquered: I do recall that El Cap seemed to be in much better condition than I was" (Harding, 2003, 44).

This climbing achievement was phenomenal in itself, "but also because it was here that two philosophies diverged and two charismatic leaders emerged to define them" (Mellor, 2001, 214). The climbing author goes on to describe that a clean kind of ascent, used on smaller crags, was thought by Robbins to be a style that could translate to the higher climbs. Harding, in contrast, and with climber Dean Caldwell, climbed "The Wall of the

Early Morning Light" in 27 consecutive days on the wall, bolting as he did so. They placed 330 bolts all told where there was no natural line to follow. In the next year, however, Robbins, with Lauria, reclimbed the same route, chopping off the bolts placed earlier by Harding. Yet on seeing that Harding had obviously also used aid skills and had not just bolted his way up the face, Robbins and Lauria left most of the route as it was. However, this split between traditionalists and the newer advocates of sport climbing has been well documented:

> Throughout the history of Yosemite climbing, an idea would split and two systems of thought would travel parallel but separate from each other. Proponents of the systems would become adversaries, and their groups would stay distrustfully apart, huddled safe at campfires of the like-minded. . . ."Valley Christians", Harding called the judgemental purists. "Vandals in the Temple," Robbins described the sport-climbers knocking on the valley door. At their ugliest, the contentions would even lead to fights. (Mellor, 2001, 216)

Another historic climb of the period was Robbins, Tom Frost, Chuck Pratt, and Yvon Chouinard's first ascent of "North America Wall," El Capitan, in 1964. This was achieved after battling fierce heat and then a storm: "As the storm rose to pass the Sierra, the rain turned to snow at 7000 feet. There we sat, in the furious, inky night, lashed by wind and rain, tiny mites tied to a great rock" (Robbins, 2003, 64). But, after a successful ascent, Robbins reported that they were all "happy as pagans" (64). The first ascent of "North America Wall" has been seen as the crown jewel of the golden age of Yosemite climbing. And because of this achievement, climbing in the United States, and especially at Yosemite, attracted much international prestige (Huber & Zak, 2003).

The first all-female ascent of El Capitan was done in 1973 by Sibylle Hechtel with Bev Johnson, when they climbed "Triple Direct." Two years later, "The Nose" was climbed (almost free) in one day by Jim Bridwell, John Long, and Billy Westbay. In 1979, Ray Jardine and Bill Price did the first-ever free ascent of a big climb on El Capitan, the west face (Roper, 1994).

Therefore, it was from the late 1950s onwards that the big-wall climbing of Yosemite was pioneered. New styles of pitons, hauling techniques, and protection devices such as nuts all helped in the 1950s and 1960s to move climbing standards and freestyle climbing on at breathtaking speed.

This ensured that Yosemite, in this period, would go down in climbing history in the United States and worldwide (see Chapter 6, "Technicalities," for information on developments in climbing gear). As the infamous Bridwell, thought by many to be the most influential climber in Yosemite, says of the era: "What could be more exhilarating than climbing steep rock uninhibited by aid gadgetry?" (Bridwell, 2003, 82).

Another important aspect of Yosemite's history was the establishment, in the 1960s, of Camp 4. Situated in the valley, it has been described as something unique to the rock-climbing scene in the United States at that period, a place where nonconformist and rebellious rock climbers hung out. In Yosemite, this new era can be seen to have begun with the first ascent of the "Lost Arrow Chimney," which was, at the time, the most difficult climb ever done. Of this time, the climber Steve Roper said, "Other remarkable climbs followed shortly, and in Camp 4, and on the great granite cliffs, I witnessed events that in later years took on mythic qualities. I strode among giants, friends tell me now, though at the time, I felt more like a misfit associating with oddballs" (Roper, 1994, 11). These climbers counted Robbins, Harding, Frank Sacherer, Pratt, Chouinard, and Powell as among the most famous at that time. (See Chapter 5, "Heroes," for biographies of some of these pioneering climbers.)

During the early 1970s, a group of young climbers from California named the Stonemasters emerged. Roper describes them as "a group of wild, honed youths from the Southland" who "made the Golden Age climbers proud" (1994, 234). Their exploits included soloing hard climbs such as "Salathé Wall," and their numbers included John Bachar, Long, Ron Kauk, Jardine, Henry Barber, and Steve Wunsch, among others (see Long & Fidelman, 2009).

Camp 4 in Yosemite has been described as a hippie subculture where drugs were the norm, including soft drugs but also LSD and mescaline. Huber and Zak (2003) recount that some climbers were high on drugs even while climbing on the big walls. However, it was in the context of the hedonistic lifestyles celebrated at Camp 4 during the 1970s that exponents such as Bachar and Kauk advanced freestyle climbing.

One instance that famously sums up the hedonistic atmosphere of Camp 4 during this period was the rumored plane crash into a nearby lake, supposedly of a plane carrying a load of marijuana. One climber during this period described the incident as "Hiking for Dollars," with some climbers hiking to the site of the crash and retrieving the marijuana and then selling the goods:

"in a week's time more than half a million dollars worth of booty had been hauled to light. Climbers who a few weeks before hadn't got two dimes to rub together, streamed back into the valley and were spending cash with all the nonchalance of a Saudi prince" (Long, cited in Huber and Zak, 2003, 72).

Furthermore, given the superb bouldering on granite that Yosemite offers, Camp 4 continued to be of historic importance. In 1984, the British climber Jerry Moffatt wrote about the classic bouldering problem "*Midnight Lightening*": "I had fulfilled a dream and was just so happy and excited. I can remember as I reached the finger jug knowing that I had done it. It was just brilliant to repeat such a classic piece of bouldering history" (cited in Huber and Zak, 2003, 100). He returned to Yosemite in 1993 with Kurt Albert, initially to free "The Nose," but was distracted by bouldering at Camp 4 again. This time, the powerful boulder problem "The Dominator" was established by Moffatt (Planet Mountain.com, 2009).

However, others see the myths that have grown up around Camp 4 as obscuring, then as now, the apathy and squalidness of the site: "Life at Camp 4 becomes a drug for many, inducing woeful apathy. Lots of bouldering. Lots of talk. Lots of plans. Not much action. For a few particularly parasitic residents, life in the Valley becomes a routine. . . . Like the bold, fat squirrels, these are a kind of park wildlife, relegated to a preserve at Sunnyside Walk-In Campground and inadvertently fed by the visitors" (Mellor, 2001, 221). Yet the myths of climbing at that time endure and can be said to continue to inspire the current generation of climbers in Yosemite.

A new surge of competitiveness and progression occurred during the mid and late 1980s, such that "every record was being systematically broken and free climbers were steadily taking over in the speed race" (Huber and Zak, 2003, 113). For example, in 1985, the Canadian Peter Croft and American John Bachar climbed El Capitan and Half Dome in one day (Huber and Zak, 2003). Arguably, free soloing in Yosemite has a higher status than anywhere else on the planet. In 1986, Wolfgang Güllich "bagged" the first solo ascent of "Separate Reality" (5.11d). In 1987, Peter Croft made an unbelievable free solo climb of "Astroman" (5.11c), a feat achieved by Dean Potter and Alex Honnold in later years (MacDonald, 2007).

A landmark achievement for women and for climbers the world over was Lynn Hill's free ascent of "The Nose" in 1993 with Brooke Sandahl. Hill was the first person to achieve this. Later, her redpointing all pitches on

"The Nose" in less than 24 hours was nothing short of phenomenal. Huber and Zak redpointed "The Headwall on the Salathé" on El Capitan (5.13b) in 1995, leading them to later claim that "The redpoint ascents of The Nose and Salathé Wall meant the spell had been lifted. Free the big walls is today the most important aspect of what is going on in the Valley" (Huber and Zak, 2003, 149).

More recently, in 2001, the UK climber Leo Houlding started his amazing and extremely ambitious venture on a new climb. His intention was to scale the southeast face of El Capitan with advice from Yosemite pioneer Bridwell and his UK climbing partner Jason Pickles. The level of difficulty inherent in this ambitious plan can be seen in their intention not to employ the usual "siege tactics" for such a climb. That is, they intended to attempt the route from the ground up, with no bolts, on sight, and with no portaledge (that is, a kind of tent system that hangs from the walls to allow a climber to sleep on the climb, over days if necessary) (Jackson, 2011a). To put this in perspective, when Houlding was 18, his first visit to the Valley in 1998 resulted in one fall on the first pitch of El Nino (5.13c), but then he did the route on sight. Years later, in 2010, he had realized his ambition and "freed" "The Prophet." This was done, he says, "With the speed-climbing skills and general understanding of big walling we had gained over five seasons in the Valley, we were no longer awestruck by the scale and logistics of climbing on the Captain" (Houlding, 2011, 48). His exploits reveal the skill, tenacity, bravery, madness, and passion needed to climb at such a level. He has spoken about how the overambitiousness of the climb affected him, for example, by his not being able to sleep or eat and even vomiting his morning coffee. However, as he finally said when the climb was successfully completed, "Unconcerned by the pain, with tape and a hit of adrenalin, I attacked *The Prophet's* final defence. . . . We collapsed into it—elated. *The Prophet* was finally free" (55).

Also climbing in 2010, the Americans Dean Potter and Sean Leary hold the current record for speed climbing on El Capitan at 2:36:45 hours. This broke Hans Florine and Yuji Hirayama's record by just 20 seconds. (In 2007, the infamous climbing brothers Alexander and Thomas Huber previously held the record with the time of 2:45:45.)

On June 22, 2010, American Alex Honnold set a rope solo record on "The Nose," posting a time of 5:49 hours. (In addition, he rope soloed the "Regular Route" on Half Dome earlier that morning, also in a record time of 2:09 hours). Other notable achievements in 2010 include the 24-year-old Nik Berry, from Sandy, Utah, free climbing El Capitan three times in a month.

However, it is not just the world's famous climbers who go to Yosemite. Recently, Lizzy Scully (2010) came up with a list of mostly obscure, moderate Yosemite climbs of very good quality that were within the range of the non-elite climber. Also, nowadays, in Tuolumne, more moderate and protected routes have sprung up than traditionally was the case: "Tuolumne has finally reached a stage where the bold and the fun can exist side by side" (Lucas, 2011, 64).

Moreover, women climbers continue to push the grades in this region. The professional climber Beth Rodden has spoken about the difficulties, in 2008, of doing "Meltdown" at Yosemite, thought to be a 5.14c climb. It was, she reported, an extremely difficult task both physically and mentally as the 70-foot crack took her over 40 days to complete. This was the longest she had ever spent on a single route (see Bisharat, 2010c). Furthermore, in 2010, it was estimated that over 100 new routes were put up on the crags at Yosemite Valley (Stephens, 2010).

In conclusion, great bouldering and sport climbing have evolved at Yosemite despite the latter once being anathema there. However, it still remains that "Long, moderate, traditional routes continue to be the focus

View of the Flatirons on the front range of Colorado. (Adam Pastula)

for most visiting climbers, and these will probably remain forever as the real Yosemite experience for most people . . . " (Mellor, 2001, 219).

colorado

Colorado's Front Range has been described as the literal edge of the Rockies and the metaphorical cutting edge of climbing in the United States. Mellor (2001) also reveals that it is an area that offers all types of rock climbing, including mountaineering and bouldering, and that has soft sandstone at the Garden of the Gods, while Eldorado Canyon features hard sandstone. Boulder Canyon also affords short cragging on granite; Lumpy Ridge offers multipitch routes on the same type of rock; there is climbing close to the road; and South Platte River consists of wild dome-land route possibilities. Indeed, as Mellor points out: "For the breadth of climbing possibilities and depth of the climbing culture, Boulder has long been seen as the original hub city of American rock climbing" (Mellor, 2001, 119).

In their classic book on rock climbing in Colorado, *Climb!* (first edition 1977, second edition 2002), the editors Achey, Chelton, and Godfrey outline how Colorado has some of the world's most advanced rock climbs. However, they also point out that routes, even if difficult, do not in themselves make for an interesting climbing history. A climbing history of any region needs people to make it come alive. They therefore argue that "Boulder has one of the largest and most intense climbing communities in the world. Other towns—Estes Park, Fort Collins, Colorado Springs, Aspen, Durango, Telluride—have their own climbing tribes, each proud and distinct. . . . Writers go to New York. Actors go to Hollywood. Climbers go to Colorado" (2002, 8). It was in this climbing area that climbers such as Ament, Jim Erickson, Dave Breashears, and Layton Kor became legends.

Colorado has both outcrops for rock climbing and literally hundreds of peaks over 13,000 feet, though there are only a few faces that could be termed big walls. Longs Peak, at 14,255 feet, is the dominant mountain in the park; East Face allows for a range of technical rock climbs in the midst of Alpine grandeur; while in the center of East Face is the Diamond. The Diamond in particular has been at the center of both climbing developments and achievements.

The geography of the region has given rise to a rich mountaineering past. In 1896, a number of Boulder hikers formed the Rocky Mountain Climbers Club, mainly meant for scrambling and hiking, and the

Colorado Mountain Club was initiated in 1912. Up until 1920, using a rope on the rock was seen as cheating. However, Rudolph Johnson, when referring to climbing the east face of the Third Flatiron in 1923 (which was the very first recorded rock climb in the state), mentions using a rope (Achey, Chelton, & Godfrey, 2002). In addition, most of the area's high peaks were climbed in the nineteenth century, while in the 1940s the largest faces of the Flatirons had routes established on them.

In the 1950s, in a similar situation to those climbers in California and on the East Coast, postwar Colorado climbers were isolated from events happening elsewhere. The author and climber Chris Jones (1997) notes this when he details how climbing skills did not develop much in the prewar years. Moreover, the region could be seen as a backwater during the 1940s and 1950s. This was at least partially due to the fact that climbers here often had an identity as mountaineers and not specifically as rock climbers. Thus, technical skills on the smaller cliffs were downplayed, and attention remained focused on peak climbing. However, as Jones pithily observes, "But mavericks arise!" (1997, 208).

In 1950, Dale Johnson, a Boulder climber, brought climbing in Colorado into the modern age. Employing a two-rope system, Johnson managed to do "Practice Roof," the first roof climbing of its type in the region. He was also an early pioneer of the use of expansion bolts. His climbs, with their pioneering belaying techniques and better ropes, would ensure that calculated risks on climbs became more common (Achey, Chelton, & Godfrey, 2002). (See Chapter 6, "Technicalities," for more detail on gear.) But it was not until later in the 1950s that, because of the growth of free climbing, climbing in Colorado moved on apace.

There is, of course, movement between climbing regions across the vast and varied territories of the United States, which is necessary for climbing areas not to remain parochial backwaters. Certain Coloradan climbers such as Harvey T. Carter and Layton Kor travelled, rather unsuccessfully, to Yosemite at that time.

Afterward, Carter wrote a letter about his experiences there to *Summit*, the first U.S. magazine to deal with climbing issues. In it, he bad-mouthed Yosemite climbers, causing a general bad feeling from them toward Coloradans for some years (Jones, 1997).

But back in Colorado, in 1959, the teaming up of Ray Northcutt with Kor, for example, on "The Diagonal" (V.5.9 A3), established what was the hardest climb in the region at that time. In so doing, Kor's exploits particularly ensured that Eldorado Canyon (at least for a while) "became the place for the aspiring Colorado hard man" (Jones, 1997, 231). When Kor traveled back to Yosemite in the 1960s, he climbed some of the hardest Yosemite cracks. But, as writers Godfrey and Chelton (1977) acknowledge, it was the Californians David Rearick and Bob Kamps, in 1960, who were to claim the first ascent of the Diamond. This was aided by their bringing out from California some new, prototype hard steel pitons, in a variety of sizes, that the climber Chouinard had been manufacturing: "After the climb, Rearick and Kamps received a 'hero's' welcome in Estes Park and found themselves star attractions in the summer rodeo parade" (Godfrey & Chelton, 1977, 97).There was also an account of the climb printed in *Time* magazine.

The 1960s have been referred to as the most important era for rock climbing in Colorado. As in other areas of the United States, Achey and colleagues (2002) note that up until around the 1950s, rock climbing had mainly been a sport that was merely a weekend activity for participants. In the 1960s, however, climbing for many was to become a complete way of life. The ending of the postwar era in the history of American climbing saw important patterns developing across California, the East Coast, and Colorado. Social mobility after the war allowed "brash newcomers" to enter the sport, and thus, "Under this new impetus, standards, techniques, and the psychological frontier were pushed ahead" (Jones, 1997, 215). Two important figures in this respect were the aforementioned Kor and Bob Culp. Kor had already made numerous first ascents in Eldorado Springs Canyon. When he teamed up with the equally fanatical Culp, they climbed routes such as the enormous and hitherto unclimbed northwest face of Chief's Head, graded 5.9 and rising around 1,500 feet. Some even saw Kor as the greatest rock climber in the country at that time (Godfrey & Chelton, 1977).

In one famous incident, Kor, along with fellow climber Jack Turner, made his way up to "Yellow Spur," Eldorado Canyon, after hearing that two kids were stuck. He found the two 16-year-olds from Boulder High School cold and huddled together in the dark on a snow-covered ledge. In fact, the boys were Larry Dalke and Pat Ament. Because of this incident, Kor, Dalke, and Ament were to become regular climbers together (Achey, Chelton, & Godfrey, 2002). Ament proclaimed, when he first arrived at the Boulder scene in 1961, that in two years he would be a better climber than Kors. However, his arrogance and ego did not always make him many friends (Jones, 1997).

In 1962, Kor and Culp climbed "Naked Edge," though it was not until 1964, with Rick Horn, that Kor returned to complete the line as climbers know it today. "Naked Edge" became one of the most classic climbs in Colorado. In later years, important developments that characterized modern free climbing were to unfold on its steep walls (Godfrey & Chelton,1977). Also in 1962, with Charles Roskosz, Kor made the second ascent of the Diamond, on "Yellow Wall." In 1963, with Robbins and in a very fast time, he put up a new climb on the Diamond, "Jack of Diamonds." In 1963, Kor, Jim McCarthy, and Tex Bossier managed the first ascent of "The Diagonal" (V 5.9 A5) in Black Canyon in just two days; the second ascent was not until 11 years later, taking 4 1/2 days (Osius, 2010).

Dalke often climbed with both Kor and Ament, so by the late 1960s he was the fastest, as well as the best, skilled aid climber in Colorado. Further, Ament and Robbins, later top-roping "Supremacy Crack," established the first 5.11 lead in in the United States, though it was not until the 1970s that climbers did this grade on sight. Kor went on to establish hard climbs with Dalke in Eldorado Canyon. Later, with Wayne Goss, in a "symbolic finish" to his exploration of Colorado, he did the first winter ascent of the Diamond. This was a two-day climb in bitter conditions and was the first winter climb of a big wall in North America. While Kor may have been Colorado's star climber, he later became a Jehovah's Witness. After this, in 1970, Bill Forrest soloed the Diamond, and, increasingly, the free climbing "revolution" after the mid 1960s was in full flow (Jones, 1997). Furthermore, Achey and colleagues (2002) note that this new style of climbing also entailed new rules to be set. These included that as few bolts as possible were to be placed, and speed was now of the essence. Climbers such as Rearick and Robbins were important in this early stage alongside Ament and Dalke.

Colorado is also a significant area in the history of bouldering. The well-known boulderer John Sherman (1994), in his book on the history of bouldering, *Stone Crusade*, recalls the early days for this style of climbing. This was a period, in the late 1950s and early 1960s, when Flagstaff Mountain above Boulder was witness to Culp being the most important boulderer there. Ament also put up difficult boulder problems, being very gifted:

Ament was climbing *Pratt's Overhang* (B-5.10) at night. He was on top, so Dalke stopped spotting him. In the dark Ament lost his balance and fell to the ground, crashing on his back. . . . Dalke jumped on him and pushed on his chest to get him breathing again. The next day Ament's wrist was in a cast. Three days later he was nailing routes in Eldorado with his left hand. (Sherman, 1994, 23)

The name of John Gill is legendary in relation to the sport of bouldering. In 1967 he moved to Colorado, pioneering bouldering on the small rocks in Georgia and Alabama. Later, Gill worked on tricks and training exercises especially for bouldering. These included a one-arm front lever and a one-finger pull up. He also introduced gymnastic chalk to rock climbers so their hands were less sweaty when used and could more easily grip the rock (Achey, Chelton, & Godfrey, 2002). The central thing for Gill was that bouldering was to be an end in itself. His influence on the sport of bouldering during the mid 1970s cannot be overestimated (Sherman, 1994). Climbers such as Jim Holloway tried to replicate Gill's strength tricks. It was at Horsetooth Reservoir, Fort Collins, Colorado, that Gill is best known for his bouldering. Later, in the 1980s, at Flagstaff and also Fort Collins, "Many of the leading boulderers from the Front Range Golden Age dropped out of the scene, which consequently lost energy" (Sherman, 1994, 35). In other areas, Sherman's boulder problems in Colorado, such as "Germ Free Adolescence," done in 1980 in Eldorado Canyon, would become classics.

In relation to rock climbing, however, things began to dramatically change in the early and mid 1980s. This was due in part to developments in places such as France, where steep limestone face climbs were protected by bolts, placed there by rappelling. Standards of free climbing were being raised. Further, in 1982, British climber Jerry Moffatt did a repeat climb of "Psycho Roof" (5.12d) at Eldorado Canyon. He also repeated "Genesis" (5.12d, First Ascent; both were first ascents of Collins in 1975 and 1979.): "The Brits' visit made it clear to local climbers that Boulder had fallen off the world pace, diluting its energy with stylistic squabbling. What was needed was less guilt and clinging to tradition, and more pure effort on the rock. This was obviously what was going on in Britain" (Achey, Chelton, & Godfrey, 2002, 178).

During this period, events were taking place in other regions of the United States that would affect traditional climbing areas such as Colorado. Siegrist (2010) details how, in this era, climbers Alan Watts, Chris Jones, and Bill Ramsey at Smith Rock State Park, Oregon, were faced with the fact that most of the aid climbs and cracks had been freed here. They therefore took up the controversial methods of "rap bolting"—fixing bolts into the rock so a climber can then use a rappel rope and "hangdogging"—hanging on a rope to be able to work out difficult climbing moves, to be able to attempt new climbs. In this area, Watts created what were possibly the United States' first sport climbs; "Watts Tots" (5.12b) and "Chain Reaction" (5.12c), leading to later great efforts such as "To Bolt or Not to Be" (the United States' first 5.14) by Beth Rodden, "Scarface" (the United States' first 5.14 climbed by an American), and "Just Do It" (5.14c): "Although Smith Rock was unquestionably the first internationally recognized American sport climbing destination, the practice of bolting routes spread like wildfire throughout the States. Even classic traditional areas such as City of Rocks and Eldorado Canyon began to see sport routes of their own" (Siegrist, 2010, para. 3).

Mellor (2001) notes that when sport climbing was emerging, Boulder was one of the very first areas to initially struggle with, but then accept, the new methods such climbing entails. The climber Christian Griffith broke with established traditions and began to put up routes in the 5.12 to 5.13 grades. This caused some outrage at the time before other such routes subsequently sprang up in different areas of Colorado. Areas such as Shelf Road and later Rifle Mountain Park were therefore established as popular sport climbing venues. Thus, as Achey and colleagues (2002) note, the preferred climbing attire was now neon Lycra tights. Moreover, climbing terminology became increasingly European with terms such as *redpointing* becoming commonplace, and climbs of the 5.13 grade were to become the norm: "By the 1990s, few road-tripping visitors would even visit Boulder, bound instead for Colorado areas yet untouched and unknown" (210).

Shelf Road was a prominent sport climbing venue in the late 1980s and early 1990s, with the crag being used as a training ground before the advent of climbing gyms. In 1998, through the Access Fund's buying Cactus Cliff, 200 new lines were put up (Baker, 2010). In a sense, a development such as this helped to democratize climbing further, as greater numbers of climbers were doing the same routes. However, such developments could be interpreted differently if seen from another viewpoint. Others have seen such climbs as a "rat race," with "a scramble for first ascents" (Achey, Chelton, & Godfrey, 2002, 211).

In the United States, the Access Fund, founded in 1991, is a national advocacy organization that aims to ensure that U.S. climbing areas are kept open and so conserve the climbing

**environment for the future. The organization represents and
supports over 2.3 million climbers in all types of climbing
(see www.accessfund.org).**

As Chapter 1, "Explanations," noted, in the 1990s, rock climbing
became both more popular and commercialized. This was through the
sponsorship of a new breed of professional climbers by outdoor-pursuits
manufacturers and the mass-market consumption of extreme sports in general. Alongside a bolting ban in areas such as the Flatirons and Eldorado
Canyon, this entailed a rapid change in the nature of climbing there.

Despite, and sometimes because of, this new, commercialized world of
rock climbing, stars continued to emerge. Tommy Caldwell, who was taught
by his father, Mike, became the first American to lead all of the pitches on
Yosemite's "Salathé Wall" (5.13b with one fall). He also established what
was at the time (2008) the hardest sport route in the United States, in
Colorado: "Kryptonite" (5.14d)—and this before the age of 21 (Kroese,
2001)!

The Boulder scene has been described thus: "eco-chic Boulder, land of
Teva sandals and herbal teas, beautiful tanned college kids and computer
nerds, rusted Volvos held together by duct tape and Phish stickers"
(Mellor, 2001, 118). And it was in the context of this kind of lifestyle in
Boulder, Colorado, that, in 2001, Caldwell climbed "The Honeymoon Is
Over" (V5.13) at Longs Peak, Colorado, with Beth Rodden belaying. In
2003, he also did "Flex Luthor" (5.14d/15a?), Fortress of Solitude,
Colorado.

The climber Jared Ogden has been described as "one of North America's
most accomplished all-around climbers. From hard free routes to steep ice to
monster big walls, he does it all" (Kroese, 2001, 149). Living in Colorado,
he spent his early career on ice and mixed climbs in areas such as Ouray,
Silverton, and Telluride. Notable achievements include first ascent of "The
Joker's Wild" (5.12c) at Telluride. In 1996, Steph Davies (with Elaine
Lee) made the first all-female ascent of the hard crack climb "Obelisk" on
the Diamond, at Longs Peak (Ament, 2002b). She has also free soloed the
Diamond four times. Such climbs helped her emerge as one of the United
States' most well-rounded rock climbers at the time.

More recently, in 2010, hard boulder problems were done at what has
been seen as Colorado's latest hot spot; Lincoln Lake (aka Wolverine
Land).This area is below the road to Mt. Evans and has an elevation of

more than 11,600 feet. At this alpine boulderfield, young stars such as Dave Graham, Daniel Woods, and many other climbers have been working on hard boulder problems, for example, successfully doing12 V13 or harder problems during the season (Woods, 2010). In 2011, Carlo Traversi made the second ascent of Woods's "The Game" in Boulder Canyon. This was the boulder problem that was famous for its suggested V16 rating in 2010 (Fox, 2011g).

When taken together, these areas reveal several parallel streams of climbing development such as free climbing, sport climbing, bolting, and the professionalization and commercialization of rock climbing. As the UK climber and academic Andrew Popp (pers. comm.) argues, developments in these regions do not form a single linear narrative of how the sport has changed over time. However, they have similar timelines, for example in relation to technical climbing. Developments in techniques emerged in each area around a similar time but then followed different trajectories reflecting sociocultural and geographical differences. This could be seen in the Gunks having a proximity to New York City, Yosemite a proximity to San Francisco, and the relative isolation of Colorado. This development is also different from that in Europe where there is a more cohesive narrative of developments in climbing within, and even between, countries. The great size of the U.S. landscape is a factor in this difference as the above geographical examples illustrate.

3.   science

the sport of rock climbing is informed by various forms of scientific knowledge. These include the geological dimension to the sport regarding the diverse rock types and formations that exist, such as granite, sandstone and limestone, as well as the science employed by early surveyors. These were some of the first people to climb the highest and most inaccessible peaks across the United States to be able to map out the terrain. Scientific knowledge also informs the physiology, techniques, and biomechanics of rock climbing, which can be seen in studies carried out on these different aspects of the sport, including the assessment, treatment, and prevention of injuries.

the rock

Climber and geologist Sarah Garlick (2009) notes that climbers climb on granite domes, sandstone towers, limestone caves, and basalt bluffs, all the while pulling on smooth pockets, crimping tiny edges, and jamming splitter cracks. This leads her to ask certain questions: "We read the rock, figuring out how to scale its features and protect its weaknesses. But why are the rocks there in the first place? How did their features form? Why are some climbing areas unique and others so similar?" (viii). For example, how can we explain why Europe has a large quantity of limestone, for instance at El Chorro, Spain, and the Verdon, in France, or why there is gritstone in the north of England? How can we understand why Australia's Grampians consist of sandstone, or why the granite big walls of Peru's Cordillera Blanca came into existence?

> **Rock is made up of minerals. For example, limestone is composed mostly of calcite and aragonite, while granite is made up of different proportions of quartz, feldspar, and small amounts of other minerals, and lighter-colored granite is more quartz**

rich. Rock can also be classified as igneous, sedimentary, and metamorphic, that is, by the way that they are formed and their diverse textures. Igneous rock has solidified from a molten or partially molten state. Further, these rocks are characterized as either extrusive or intrusive. Extrusive rocks are characterized as basalt, andesite, and rhyolite while granite and diorite are classed as intrusive. For sedimentary rocks, both erosion and deposition help form this type of rock. This can be done through the action of wind or ice, for example. Rocks formed through such processes include shale, sandstone, limestone, and conglomerate. In addition, metamorphic rock is created through heat, pressure, or chemical action of gases or fluids. These types of rock include schist, gneiss, slate, and phyllite (Utah Geological Survey, 2011).

To understand rock formation, it is vital to understand the relatively new and debated theory of plate tectonics. This shows that the earth's surface is made up of a series of large plates, which, although they are in constant motion, only travel a few centimeters every year. In addition, the world's ocean floors are always moving. Convection currents, which are located below the plates, move them in differing directions. Furthermore, what drives these convection currents is, in fact, radioactive decay that occurs deep within the earth (Earth Science for Moorland School, n.d., para. 1). There are three primary kinds of tectonic plate boundaries: divergent boundaries, convergent boundaries, and transform boundaries (PlateTectonics.com, 2010, para. 1).

Convergent boundaries are formed at subduction zones and via continent-continent collisions. Garlick (2009) further notes that the convergent-boundary subduction zones are where two tectonic plates converge and, in time, reach the earth's surface as volcanoes. Convergent-boundary continent-continent collisions, after two continental plates have converged over time, give rise to large mountain chains as well as a very thick continental crust (Garlick, 2009). Meanwhile, divergent boundaries—midocean ridges characterized by plates moving away from each other—eventually produce a new oceanic crust through magma pushing through along the boundaries. Last, there are transform boundaries, where two tectonic plates are able to slide past each other, often producing a big strike-slip fault alongside two bounda-ries. This leads to transform boundaries in oceans and to continental transform boundaries, resulting in regions such as the Californian San Andreas Fault.

Important for rock climbers and mountaineers is that different types of boundaries produce different types of mountains and rock formations and thus directly influence the climbing experience. The Himalayas and Mount Everest are prime examples of continent-to-continent collision:

> Millions of years ago India and an ancient ocean called the Tethys Ocean were sat on a tectonic plate. This plate was moving northwards towards Asia at a rate of 10 centimeters per year. The Tethys oceanic crust was being subducted under the Asian Continent. The ocean got progressively smaller until about 55 million years ago when India "hit" Asia. There was no more ocean left to lubricate the subduction and so the plates welled up to form the High Plateau of Tibet and the Himalayan Mountains. (Earth Science for Moorland School, n.d., para. 5)

The geography in the Himalayan mountains thus lends itself to mountaineering on big peaks, which need snow-and-ice climbing techniques, with big expedition climbing being common.

The climbing area of Yosemite serves as an interesting case study that reveals how a specific type of rock was formed in a particular location and so influences the type of climbing that can be performed there. In Yosemite Valley, as well as the adjoining uplands, the forces of erosion have exposed a very complex assemblage of granitic rocks. These consist of a number of different minerals, including between 20 and 60 percent quartz. In addition, the rocks that are the walls and domes of the Yosemite Valley area, which belong to the Sierra Nevada, originated from molten material—magma—that existed miles below the earth's surface. It took millions of years for the cooling and crystallization of this hidden magma to occur (King Huber & Roller, 2004). The Sierra Nevada was formed via glacial movement. From deep down in the earth, the rock was "pushed to the surface by the forces of plate tectonics and stripped by erosion of thousands of feet of softer rock that had overlain the granite. Once exposed to the surface, the rock's form was largely determined by joint patterns" (Mellor, 2001, 199).

The joint patterns referred to are parallel fractures. Those who climb in areas such as Yosemite are thus often termed "crack climbers." Climbing on such fractured surfaces involves the use of specific techniques such as laybacking, or jamming up a crack to ascend a route. It is these geological developments and the diverse rock formations resulting from them that have ensured that specific physical environments require different

El Capitan, Yosemite National Park, California. (Mariusz Jurgielewicz | Dreamstime.com)

climbing techniques and styles. Climbers are forced to respond to the rock's features in different ways. In Wyoming, for instance, "Devil's Tower demands that you can stem like a gymnast. Southern sandstone rewards the climber with fingers of steel and lats like a flying squirrel. And Utah's canyon climbing wants a soft touch, for on some routes you can scratch your initials into the rock with your fingernails" (Mellor, 2001, 12). This directly influences the climbing experience, as U.S. climber Kaydee Summers (pers. comm.) notes in relation to climbing on sandstone, which can be "hard to climb" as it sometimes feels "as if a hold will break off at any given moment and it is actually 'a scary thing' when you feel the rock crumble in your fingers."

However, Garlick (2009) complicates the idea that there are automatic correlations between particular climbing movements and specific rock types. In fact, certain rock features such as pockets, cracks, and corners are found in different types of rock. However, she also recognizes that some types of rock and environmental conditions lead to specific features being more prevalent. Therefore, granite landforms are often shaped like domes and lead to slab climbing, while slopers are often formed when rock corners or edges become rounded over time, most often by a process of chemical weathering.

In a practical sense, climbers are concerned with issues that either prevent or enable them to rock climb, including both the geology of the rock (as indicated above) and the effects of society's intervention on the natural environment. For example, some scientists contend that global warming is causing Europe's mountains to become taller. This is said to be due to heavy glaciers, which are causing the earth's crust to flex inward a little. This means that when glaciers disappear, the crust actually springs back and the mountains are, however slowly, pushed upwards (Than, 2006). Other issues that affect where and how climbers can pursue their sport are factors such as coastal erosion, which affects the potential to climb on sea cliffs, and human activity such as quarrying. For instance, the Auburn State Recreation Area in the Sacramento region of California reveals that though the geographical or geological location of an area may be suited for climbing, access issues may prevent this. Apparently, the rock left behind after quarrying, which is highly featured limestone and other sedimentary rock, is well suited for climbing, but it is not legal at the site (Rockclimbing.com, 2011).

early geological climbers

In 1860, the California legislature established the Geological Society. Keen to conduct a survey of the whole of California, the scientist and geologist Josiah Dwight Whitney played a key role in developing the society (Jones, 1997). In 1862, with his assistant William Brewer, Whitney climbed Mount Shasta, a volcanic mountain in the north, with barometers specifically made for the task, to assess if it was the highest peak in the land. The young geologist Clarence King, enthused by Whitney and Brewer's exploits, eventually climbed Mount Whitney, claiming to find a cairn on the summit that had an arrow shaft through it. Whether this discovery was true or not, arrowheads had most certainly been found over the whole of the Sierra, and so "Although these findings are no proof that Indians climbed the peaks, they are strong supporting evidence" (Jones, 1997, 34). Amusingly, when King realized he had initially climbed the wrong Mount Whitney, he proceeded to climb the right mountain, though three other parties had already climbed it the same year! Later, women, under the guise of being botanists, also scaled some of the highest peaks in the United States.

The Scottish American John Muir (1838–1914) was to make many successful summits, including Yosemite's Cathedral Peak, after he first visited the area in 1868. As the British academic and climber Terry Gifford (1992) recounts, Muir was not just a geologist but a botanist, mountaineer, instinctive ecologist, and lobbyist. In 1871, Muir's very first article was published in the *New York Tribune*, in which he argued that Yosemite Valley had been formed by the slowly evolving process of glaciation. Although many, including Whitney and King, doubted his claims, Muir's glacialization theory was ultimately proved correct. Muir actively campaigned for protection of the Yosemite Valley, which become the first protected state park in 1864. In 1890, it was declared a national park, thus making it the second oldest in the world after Yellowstone Park. Muir also founded the Sierra Club in 1892 "to promote understanding of nature and safeguard its originality" (Huber & Zak, 2003, 29).

By 1900, many of the most prominent mountains in the United States had been climbed, often by surveyors and geologists such as Whitney, Brewer, King, and Muir. But these early surveyors, scientists, and other adventurers of the mid-nineteenth century were usually climbing for work purposes rather than as a leisure pursuit or personal challenge; the climbing experience in itself "was often a onetime thing" (Jones, 1997, 43). Therefore, such exploits could not be technically classed as mountaineering, and it was those who came later possessing both leisure time and a need to take risks who were to build upon the scientific discoveries and knowledge of rock formations through advancing the sport of rock climbing and mountaineering.

physiology, techniques, and biomechanics

With the support of the British Mountaineering Council, the first International Conference on Science and Technology in Climbing and Mountaineering was held in 1999 at the University of Leeds (UK). Papers were given on different aspects of science and technology that could be applied to the study and performance of climbing and mountaineering, for example on textiles, equipment design, biomechanics, sports injury, physiology, environmental factors, climbing-wall design, climbing safety, and coaching/training science. The physiological dimensions of climbing are important for understanding how the human body reacts to the rigors of climbing as well as the techniques and biomechanics inherent in rock climbing. Also of growing interest is the science and technology of different types of equipment, from ropes and helmets to textiles and clothing, required to make climbing both safer and more effective regarding an individual's performance. (For the technology of clothing, see Chapter 6,

"Technicalities.") There have also been studies that look at climbing injury and rehabilitation, as this chapter goes on to demonstrate, as well as research on how climbing can benefit children's physical fitness levels (Baláš, 2005).

In a review of the UK conference proceedings published in the *Australian Journal of Outdoor Education*, Mark Smith writes,

> My climbing mate and I are built differently: he is shorter with a well-developed upper body profile; I am taller and some 20 kilograms heavier. We warm up differently, move on the rock differently and probably think about climbing differently ... although we do tend to use the same excuses on those days when the body will not perform as its mind would wish. Talk often covers the topic of the various physiological advantages that our respective bodies allow us—talk which is as much out of ignorance as wishful thinking. (2000, para. 1)

The question on Mark's, and many other climbers', mind is, of course, "What is it that makes a good climber?" Crucial to this question is the issue of the differing physiological and metabolic responses in different climbers. Smith notes that the conference proceedings outlined six variables in assessing climbing performance. These are (1) the background conditions such as time and talent; (2) any external conditions regarding the type of rock and the equipment the climber has; (3) aspects such as experience, knowledge, and goals that could be defined as tactical; (4) psychological traits, which could include arousal, fear, and the ability to concentrate; (5) pure climbing coordination and technique; and last, (6) strength, power, endurance, and flexibility, which can be defined as an individual climber's own physical abilities.

These are all aspects of climbing explored by researchers since the late 1980s. As Vomáčko (2005) points out, with the rise of sport climbing and its attendant minimization of danger, and the potential this gives for harder routes, the physical form of a climber is more important than ever. Sport climbing can take place indoors on artificial holds, or outside, with very different inclination of angles, and a climber's motor skills and abilities are of paramount importance. This has lead to an increasing number of empirical studies where climbers are tested, in different climbing situations, on differing variables and for reasons ranging from a desire to help climbers' performance to a need for knowledge about injury prevention. Many of the studies conducted during the first half of the 1990s and later explained climbing performance as largely determined by anthropometric indicators (that is, the measurement of a human being) (See Watts, Martin, and Durtschi, 1993; Grant et al., 2001). Simultaneously, other studies examined the psychological factors contributing to performance in terms of focus and motivation, for instance, with some particularly focusing on young climbers (Sarrazin et al., 2002).

Physiologists have examined how sport-climbing performance is affected by a local aerobic metabolism (Vomáčko, 2005). A study in 2000 by Watts and colleagues was concerned to assess metabolic responses of rock climbers and the effects of an active or a passive recovery after climbing. The results showed that handgrip strength was significantly decreased at 1 minute postclimb for the active-recovery climbers but did not change very much for those assigned passive recovery. The study also concluded that low-intensity active recovery significantly reduced any accumulated blood lactate within 20 minutes following difficult climbing, which would likely minimize the feelings of fatigue following a big climb. Another study concerned with the energy expenditure and physiological responses of indoor rock climbers showed that indoor rock climbing certainly increases both muscular endurance and cardiorespiratory fitness (Mermier, Roberg, McMinn, & Heyward, 1997).

Researchers have also been interested in the anthropometric profiles of elite and competitive male and female rock climbers. In general, elite sport climbers tend to have very low body fat, are often of small to moderate stature, and have a moderate grip strength but also a high grip-strength-to-body-mass ratio, if compared to other sporting groups. Another study showed that the body parts that receive the most exercise during climbing have the most developed muscles, particularly the areas of the shoulder girdle and the upper extremities, with muscles also being developed on the forearms (Vomáčko, 2005). The bodies of many climbers seen either at the local climbing gym or climbing outside certainly support this study, with committed climbers displaying well-developed upper extremities. Many climbers develop the upper body at the expense of the lower so that, stereotypically, skinny legs can often be seen on rock climbers in comparison to overdeveloped shoulders, for example.

While there is a typical climbing physique, in reality there are variations of different body types even among top climbers. A poster on a climbing website, for example, illustrates these differences in a discussion of the bodies of two superstar climbers, the American Chris Sharma and the Czech Adam Ondra:

> From what I recall, Sharma tends to milk rests (even mediocre ones) and spends a good amount of time looking ahead and checking out the coming moves. He also climbs much less efficiently than Ondra is capable of. Of course he does all those things at points, but I've never seen a video of a Sharma onsight that was even remotely similar. He has a completely different body type and climbing style. He's been at the top of climbing for more than a decade, but Ondra is clearly moving the next generation ahead. (Lipinski, 2011, para. 26)

From this it can, therefore, be concluded that Sharma can be seen as having a mesomorph body type with a thicker bone structure and putting on muscle weight more easily than other types. With an ectomorph body type, Ondra is very tall and thin. Sharma needs muscle to enable him pull his weight up, whereas Ondra, weighing less, does not need lots of muscle mass to allow him to do the same. Furthermore, weight as a body factor in and of itself is not necessarily a barrier to climbing well. Increased weight in a climber means more strength and power. And of course, with sufficient will power, it can be controlled!

Other scientific studies have been concerned with body type, strength, endurance, and flexibility of rock climbers. For instance, in 1996, scientists from the Institute of Biomedical and Life Sciences, University of Glasgow (UK), compared the body shape and size, strength, endurance, and flexibility of elite and recreational climbers to those who were nonclimbers but were physically active in other sporting or exercise forms (Grant et al., 1996). This was achieved through diverse tests such as assessing body composition, body dimensions, different types of finger strength, arm strength and endurance, flexibility, and abdominal endurance. The results overall showed that it was the elite group of climbers who have more shoulder-girdle endurance, finger strength, and hip flexibility, and not the recreational climbers or nonclimbers. The authors' recommendations to those wanting to climb at harder levels were to incorporate shoulder-girdle strength and endurance, finger strength, and hip flexibility exercises into individual training schedules.

What does this scientific research mean for everyday climbers who want to improve their sporting performance or are concerned to minimize any potential for climbing injuries? How do climbers access this sort of information, and how does it inform their training and climbing practices? Climbing publications often have regular columns that are focused on optimizing sporting performance for climbers but that also give advice from those medically qualified on specific climbing injuries. For example, some climbers need to get "pumped up" as part of their warmup routine when on-sighting a climb. Psychologists refer to this as getting into the zone of optimal functioning by increasing arousal levels. (In this context, to be "pumped" means to have sufficient energy and excitement to be able to climb effectively.) Advice from the climbing coach Neil Gresham (2009) is to get moderately "pumped" in a very controlled way before attempting to on-sight the climb in question. This way, you recruit more muscle fibers, preparing yourself for the harder moves needed on a more difficult climb, and summoning up the mindset and techniques needed for the task at hand.

Another example of scientific knowledge filtering down to the everyday climber can be seen in the advice given to a climber who had sustained a finger injury while climbing at Hueco Tanks, Texas. The climber concerned needed information about the use of anti-inflammatory medication to reduce swelling: "Non-steroidal anti-inflammatory drugs (NSAIDs) are bandied around like Halloween Candy. Though I would love to have some ammunition to discourage their widespread use, not a shred of reasonable evidence says that the short-term use of NSAIDs has a significant effect on fracture healing, though many web pages report that they do" (Saunders, 2010, 72). Advice pages such as these are an important medium to enable the rock climber to make informed choices about his or her sporting health, especially given the enormous amount of conflicting information sources available to climbers in the digital age.

injuries

Studies concerned with the performance capabilities of climbers often assess injury rates, types, and prevention measures. For instance, Wright, Royle, and Marshall (2001) examined the frequency of injuries sustained by indoor climbers as well as the sites where such injuries happened. They were concerned with what elements conspire to help or reduce the probabilities of any given climber having an overuse injury when training in a certain way. To assess this, they used a questionnaire to look at overuse injury in 295 spectators and competitors who were all at the 1999 Entre-Prises World Climbing Championships held in Birmingham, UK. They found that 44 percent of participants had sustained an overuse injury, most usually in the finger, and in certain groups (i.e., men, climbers who had climbed for over 10 years and climbers who lead harder routes or boulder). Perhaps not surprisingly, they concluded that those rock climbers who have more ability and are more dedicated to the sport face the probability of more overuse injuries. The key point here is that climbers who are aware of this can take steps to avoid such injury, for instance, or can be more aware of the signs and symptoms of such injuries once they happen.

Another study, conducted by scientists from the Division of Orthopedic Surgery, Duke University Medical Center, Durham, North Carolina, revealed the prevalence of arm-muscle injuries in climbing (Koukoubis et al., 1995). According to the researchers, if we know the activity of specific muscles when climbing, training programs can be designed to reduce injuries within specific muscle groups.

It is also acknowledged that variables other than the physiological can affect a climber's performance and, therefore, his or her susceptibility to injury. The relationship between agility, climbing performance, and length of climbing practice has been studied in this context. Observing the performances of 18 participants of both sexes who were competing in the 2003 Czech Cup, the researcher revealed the importance of considering the psychological dimensions of performance and the value of longer climbing practice (Vomáčko, 2005). This study showed that

> The longer you climb, the more psychically resistant you become. Climbing is psychologically a very complicated activity, in which several aspects can take part: cognitive processes (perception, imagination, and attention), emotions (fear, joy) and motivation processes. An important part of the climbing practice is the consolidation of volitional qualities, such as ambition, self-control, self-confidence, courage, steadiness, etc. (Vomáčko, 2005, 93)

Climbing performance is both a technical issue (for example, learning new climbing movements) and involves tactical preparation (for example, making the right decision when to rest or place a quick-draw). However, these aspects have to be considered in relation to the variables discussed above, as well as the experience, age, and sex of the climber and his or her strength and endurance levels, which all contribute to the climber's performance and tendency to injury.

Interestingly, this study also showed that women climbers use their agility, balance, and mobility to affect climbing performance more positively than do men. Women also use these advantages to compensate for any lack of physical strength through greater coordination and better technique. The researcher also concludes that men compensate for a lower level of coordination abilities through sheer physical strength. However, it was pointed out that with such a small study, the temptation to generalize the findings to all male and female climbers should be resisted.

Also, the view that the physiological dimension of climbing cannot be separated from the psychological can be further demonstrated by the example of a climber who may be exceptionally strong but continually underperforms and does not achieve the climbing grade he or she would like to, in comparison to a physically weaker climber who consistently overperforms in terms of the grade he or she achieves. Belief in one's own climbing ability and the will to succeed can give a weaker climber the competitive edge. Sports psychologists Llewellyn and colleagues (2008), in a study of self-efficacy, risk taking, and performance in rock climbing, found that both indoor and outdoor climbers may take calculated additional risks, climb more frequently, and attempt harder climbs when they are confident in their own abilities. The researchers also point out that it should not be assumed that there is behavioral or psychological homogeneity between groups of risk takers such as climbers. Llewellyn and Sanchez (2007) also found that those climbers who were high in self-efficacy and who were male were likely to take greater risks.

Injury prevention or treatment is one of the most frequent topics to be found on climbing forums or in magazines. For example, the advice given to a climber inquiring about a chipped ankle to the climbing magazine *Rock and Ice*'s resident doctor was clear: "You dislocated your ankle. You are going to suffer. A few bone chips are the least of your concerns. These will be minor avulsion fractures caused by the ligaments on the outside of your ankle, tearing bone off instead of snapping mid-substance" (Saunders, 2011, 70). The verdict is that the "soft- tissue carnage" sustained by the climber means that it may take up to a year to recover from the injury, provided the climber works at it. This means exercises to increase ankle mobility, an ankle brace, and taping up the ankle. The final piece of advice is to "Get some professional help." However, no matter how careful a climber is in warming up or avoiding taking unnecessary risks, for instance, sometimes injuries are inevitable. This can be seen especially as a climber gets older, when hand, fingers, wrist, shoulder, and elbow injuries are commonplace because of overuse over time.

To date, many studies have examined the physiological, technical, biomechanical, and psychological dimensions of climbing separately. Smith

(2000) argues that establishing the importance of personality types and reasons for climbing would further complicate such an assessment, as was outlined in Chapter 1. Arguably, we need a sociological perspective, as well an awareness of physiological and psychological factors, to be able to fully assess the reasons why different people climb, how frequently they do so, and at what levels of prowess and commitment. The science and technology of rock climbing can also be demonstrated in looking at the gear and equipment climbers use, as well as their various training routines and practices, as Chapter 6, "Technicalities," demonstrates.

4. places and events

this chapter is concerned with some of the important events and sites that shaped and changed the face of American rock climbing over the past decades and up to the present. A number of these places were introduced initially in earlier chapters. Some of these areas have gone in and out of fashion while others are today's hot spots, places to be seen at or to visit on a climbing road trip.

> For a time, one particular climbing region will take on almost mythic proportions. It will seem like the center of a universe. The magazines will focus on its local heroes, whose names and accomplishments will float bigger than life across the nation and into conversations around campfires. Climbers will pack their vans and make the pilgrimages. ... But the earth's axis remains unsteady, and the poles continue to wander. (Mellor, 2001, 43)

As the Preface indicated, climbing is a global practice, and the style of climbing as well as the techniques required to climb on a specific type of rock are determined by different things. These can include the geology of a region, weather conditions, and the history, local traditions, and ethics of rock climbing in different countries. Different countries have, over time, established themselves as climbing meccas. This is illustrated in regions as diverse as Asia, with climbing on limestone in Thailand; sandstone cliffs in Australia; and gritstone in the north of England, where traditional climbing is paramount. The recent travel itinerary of the U.S. climber Ethan Pringle (aged 24) reveals how today's climbers (or at least those who can afford it or are sponsored by climbing companies) can be part of a climbing "global village." In 2010, after climbing in Yangshuo in China, he put up "Spicy Dumpling," which, if confirmed at 5.14d, will be China's hardest route as of March 2011. But his plans do not stop there. In this same period, Pringle was climbing in the American Southwest, "with plans to travel to Spain in the spring, and then Rocklands (South Africa), followed by Yosemite in the fall" (Fox, 2011h, 16).

A recent trawl through the United States' rock-climbing press reveals articles on climbing around the globe. For example, a Petzl superteam of around 50 top athletes from all over the world has recently been on a climbing trip in Mexico. Here, they found 600-foot limestone tufa and stalactite caves in the silver-mining town of Taxco, located two hours southwest of Mexico City, and in Jilotepec, two hours northwest of the city, where climbs are very technical and serious on conglomerate rock (Tower, 2011). In the 2011 annual photo edition of *Urban Climber*, there are essays on rock climbing in Wellington, New Zealand, and Caracas, Venezuela. In the March 2011 issue of *Climbing*, there are photo features on the climbing routes "Astro Logger" and "High Plains Drifter," both in British Columbia, Canada. In the same edition of the magazine, there are features on the top U.S. boulderer, Paul Robinson, storming through an incredible amount of boulder problems of V13 and above in Switzerland and Fontainebleau, France. Further features are present on ice climbing in Nepal, new routes in China, and climbing in Spain, where an article highlights the 1,800-foot granite slabs at La Pedriza, an hour northwest of Madrid, in marked contrast to Spain's popular sport routes at Siurana or the limestone cliffs at the Costa Blanca.

Meanwhile, in another U.S. climbing magazine, *Rock and Ice*, recent articles have featured islands in Norway with their granite routes ranging from 2,000 to 2,500 feet, rumored to be like Yosemite in quality (July 2011), ice climbing on the north face of Mount Alberta, in the Canadian Rockies (June 2009), deep-water soloing at Krabbi, Thailand (September 2010), and climbing in Mongolia on large granite walls and domes (December 2010).

Undoubtedly, therefore, there is a proliferation of climbing regions worldwide that can offer diverse styles of rock climbing in abundance. However, the claim that the United States can offer the very widest range of different kinds of climbing experience can probably be borne out by a more detailed look at its great terrain and the different sites and events that now take place. No short chapter such as this can detail all the rock-climbing areas in the United States, especially as new areas are being developed all the time. Therefore, how to classify these areas is an interesting question due to the sheer magnitude of the United States. Furthermore, as journalist Macdonald observes,

In the last year, I've been to at least eight crags I'd never climbed at before, without ever leaving the state of Colorado. Most of these cliffs have been newly developed for climbing—or have seen major infusions of new activity—in the last five years. True, Colorado has an almost absurd abundance of rock to climb. But the fact that it's possible to find eight new crags in a year, anywhere, vividly demonstrates that exploration in climbing is alive and well. (2011a, 10)

In addition to climbing areas being newly developed, it is also the case that specific rock-climbing sites gain a collective reputation over the years, which climbers may then attempt to refute, and which thus affects who climbs there. The climbing journalist Averbeck argues, "If you've spent any time in the South, you've heard the same old story: Colorado has Rifle and its public beta classes, California has the Valley and its speed junkies, and the Deep South has its secret Edens of virgin sandstone—a quarter of which may be real rock, with the rest being overhanging rumors" (2011, 40).

Access is another issue that can affect the climbing done in any given area and when it can take place. Averbeck (2011) also refers to the Chattanooga climbing region in Tennessee, where there is no national forest land, for example: "Instead, our serpentine gorges and rock-rimmed plateaus are subdivided by barbed wire and gates that proudly display *Private Property* in bright neon-orange" (40). Thus, as he points out, if any climbing areas have been kept secret, this is often done for very pragmatic reasons. Indeed, at Deep Creek, near Chattanooga, no guide book existed as of 2011 because access to the cliffs had only recently been secured. (See Chapter 7, "Futures," for more on access issues.)

The weather is also an obvious factor in deciding where and when to climb. Therefore, both temperature, or how hot or cold it has been, and what the average rainfall has been for any given area are important to note in making any climbing decisions as to the site or the best type of climbing to engage in. For example, the best time to climb at Yosemite and Bishop is seen as being the fall because winters are mostly too cold, while spring is wet and the summers are very hot.

In this chapter, three of the key climbing sites in the United States are discussed: the Shawangunks, Yosemite, and Colorado. This is followed by an examination of some of the other sites specific to the various styles of participation, including sport climbing, traditional climbing, bouldering, ice climbing, indoor climbing and competitions for diverse climbing activities.

the "big three"

The point is made above that no one chapter could do justice to or cover in enough depth the diversity of regions, both past and present, where different types of climbing takes place. With this in mind, in Chapter 2, "Origins," the three areas comprising the Shawangunks, Yosemite, and Colorado served as case studies to explore some of the key stylistic, technical, and cultural developments in the past, and to some extent the present, U.S. rock-climbing scene. These three areas are still seen as important places to visit for any climber's rite of passage.

It has been said that so many climbers live in Colorado because of the quality and proximity of the rock and the sheer number of pitches (not to mention the sunshine to be had when visiting Denver, Colorado Springs, and Boulder). The fact also remains that the elevation of Boulder makes it an extremely beneficial area for training.

> **To demonstrate why so many climbers head for Colorado, climbing writer Peters notes,**
>
> If you keep getting foiled by other parties on your alpine objectives, head over to Chaos Canyon for amazing granite bouldering. For alpine climbing and bouldering close to Denver, head to Mt. Evans. After driving (!) to over 12,000 feet, you can fulfill your trad desires on the Black Wall or feed your bouldering addiction at one of Evans' many world-class bouldering areas. (2011, 40)

Current Colorado hot spots include South Platte, where there are over 2,000 routes on granite, such as "The Classic Dihedral" (5.7) and "Wunsch's Dihedral" (5.11), which afford sport climbing, multipitch slab and crack routes, as well as single-pitch traditional-climbing classic climbs. Further, at Colorado, in the high desert at Shelf Road there is an abundance of vertical limestone climbing on moderate sport route grades 5.9 to 5.11, including "Back to the Future" (5.11c). This is a place that "has a timeless beauty that has outlasted the old arguments over style and ethics" (Baker, 2010, 63).

Regarding the Northeast, the Shawangunks are still recommended for "mega-traditional" climbing and bouldering (even if very popular): "It's still the most talked about trad and bouldering destination in America's

Margaret Wheeler, right, president of the American Mountain Guides Association, and executive director Betsy Winter, left, prepare for a costumed event in the guides' version of the Olympics during the association's 2011 conference at the Shawangunk climbing area in New Paltz, New York. (Ascent Services Worldwide LLC, Joe Lentini/AP/Wide World Photos)

upper right-hand side for a reason" (Scheinbaum, 2011, 42). Such reasons include "The Gill Egg" (V4) and roof climbing on "The Yellow Wall" (5.11c). Elsewhere in the Northeast area, the crimps, jugs, and tufa-like pinches of the sport-climbing mecca of Rumney, New Hampshire, with routes such as "Predator" (5.13b), are recommended. In addition, no trip to the Northeast would be complete without visiting North Conway and sampling the climbing to be found on the granite walls at Cathedral Ledge with its multipitch trad routes. This area has been described as "a miniature Yosemite" with routes such as the classic "Thin Air," a four-pitch climb graded 5.6 (Scheinbaum, 2011, 43). The British climber known only as "Sammy" (pers. comm.), demonstrated the global appeal of the Cathedral Ledge region when he made some daring ascents of climbs already established at the time, in the 1990s.

The other area that was originally looked at in the "Origins" chapter, Yosemite, is still lauded for being the home of the celebrated El Capitan and also of other celebrated climbing areas: "the crown jewel of Western Climbing, is only part of what Yosemite has to offer, and Bishop and the

Yosemite National Park in California, one of the most popular sites in the National Park system. (Karl Sterne)

Bay Area are stacked with places to climb" (Van Leuven & Summit, 2011, 46). Yosemite National Park, on the other hand, allows in just one day the chance to engage in sport, trad climbing on big walls, and bouldering. This is revealed, for example, by being able to summit Half Dome by "Snake Dike" (5.7R) in the valley itself or attempt "Grenade Launcher" (5.12c) at Puppy Dome in Tuolumne Meadows, "where everyone lines up nightly to watch the sun set over the granite domes" (47). Moreover, at the Bishop area in the Sierra foothills, there is Owens River Gorge (where sport climbing abounds, for example, at the Eldorado Roof and Dilithium Crystal areas) and Buttermilks, the Happys, and the Sads for bouldering. Owens River Gorge has been seen as the best sport-climbing area in California, which fell out of but is now back in fashion. The latest guidebook for this site gives more than 50 routes the highest star rating (Thornburg, 2009).

climbing "hot spots"

A number of diverse and famous climbing areas are highlighted by Mellor (2001) for affording different types of excellent climbing possibilities. These include the Adirondack and White Mountain granite, and its New

England traditionalism; the red sandstone towers of the desert Southwest, where sport climbing abounds; the steep walls and overhanging sandstone of the Southeast; the Shawangunks; crack climbing in Indian Creek and the vast canyons of Utah; Western big-wall climbing, which takes place on the white walls of Sierra granite; as well as high-altitude mountaineering in the Cascades, Tetons, and Rockies. I will now examine some of these regions as examples of contemporary climbing hot spots.

One way of classifying rock-climbing regions is by using criteria such as the popularity or beauty of any given area. Yosemite National Park, California, Joshua Tree National Park, California, and Black Canyon in Gunnison National Park, Colorado, could be seen as the top three national parks for climbing based on those criteria. However, such "hot lists," especially when broken down into individual climbing sites, are debatable. This is due to how quickly new areas are developed or older areas go in and out of fashion, not to mention how one individual's hot spot is another climber's crag nightmare! This is shown by how climbers have different preferences for the type of rock climbed on; while some appreciate crack climbing, others prefer slabs or alpine routes.

Another way of assessing or making a case for any areas' best climbs is through the production of guide books by climbers themselves. These often give specific climbs star ratings. Such ratings can assess both the level of difficulty of a climb and the quality of a route. Also, books are produced by climbers that are effectively compilations of classic routes. These include, in the United States, Steve Roper and Alan Steck's (1997) *Fifty Classic Climbs of North America* and Mark Kroese's (2001) *Fifty Favorite Climbs: The Ultimate North American Tick List*. In the United Kingdom, a book that itself has become a classic in the field is Ken Wilson's (2007) *Classic Rock: Great British Rock Climbs* (second edition). Many other countries have their own such collections, though some would argue that such compilations are subjective and run the risk of excluding other, equally classic climbs. Another argument against them is that they can cause certain climbing areas to be overpopulated with those eager to tick off a climb for their own personal hit list. However, it could equally be argued that these books have inspired generations of climbers, young and old, to venture out onto the rock and, further, that many of the routes included are indeed classics. A more contemporary and immediate successor to such books are the "hot list" five-star new-route lists compiled in the climbing press. For example, see *Climbing*,

March 2011, which included routes in the High Sierra, California; Smith Rock, Oregon; Joshua Tree, California; and Squamish, British Columbia.

Further, there are changes over time in relation to which areas and crags are seen as the "in" places to climb or not. Particular types of climbing, for instance big-wall climbing, sport climbing, or bouldering, go in and out of fashion among passionate climbers. In addition, climbing gyms and indoor climbing competitions, which previously did not exist, now proliferate across the whole of the United States. Despite these shifts and changes, however, it is still possible to note how certain areas' popularity endures, as well as their historical significance.

bouldering sites

Bouldering, defined as climbing on large boulders without ropes, is the subject of John Sherman (1994) in his classic book *Stone Crusade: A Historical Guide to Bouldering in America*. In this work, he argues that no other country on earth can equal the United States for the geographical diversity of its developed boulder fields. He outlines how bouldering sites occur from the sea cliffs of Maine to Southern California's beaches and everywhere in between these places. Also, the actual rock to boulder on includes pocketed limestone, soft sandstone, quartzite, and granite, and people boulder on toppled volcanic pillars and inside lava tubes:

> We can climb a lone glacial erratic stranded in the Yellowstone forest or gaze at boulders stretching as far as the eye can see from Mount Woodson. We have urban pockets like Stoney Point in Los Angeles, where you can gag on rush-hour smog as you boulder. We also have boulder-choked canyons on Colorado's Western Slope where you can go days without seeing another human. (1994, xxv)

Further, he documents the importance in bouldering's history of the Hueco Tanks area in Texas. In 1989 and 1990, Sherman wrote a guidebook for the region, and the scene then changed very dramatically so that high-quality bouldering was now done over the entire park. The proliferation of many three-star problems in all the grades there ensured Hueco Tanks was central to the "Golden Age" of bouldering.

John Gill, as noted in Chapter 5, "Heroes," was the founder of American bouldering and is famed for applying gymnastic techniques and gymnastic chalk to rock climbing. He bouldered in areas such as the

Tetons, the Black Hills' Needles, and the mid-South as well as at Horsetooth Reservoir, Colorado, where, along with Pat Ament, many of his classics were achieved in the late 1960s. But where are the current bouldering hot spots?

A case could be made for alpine bouldering in Colorado as an area where, in recent times, an international set of boulderers have come "to test their powers on the blocs and lungs on the hikes" (Segal, 2010, 45). This is an area where many blog sites around the world reveal how count-less new "V-hards" have been established. However, such popularity can have its downside, as Segal also observes, "Holy Shit! Where did all those people come from?" (10), referring to a visit he made to the newly redis-covered bouldering hot spot of Lincoln Lake, Mt. Evans. (This is an area where young boulderers such as Dave Graham and Daniel Woods are cur-rently doing V15 boulder problems.) In an effort to seek out new boulder-ing pastures, Segal ventured to the Sawtooths, situated in central Idaho and known more for the granite mountain Elephant's Perch and for its tra-ditional climbing than for bouldering, but with great potential for first ascents to still be done.

Other fashionable, and thus much-visited, bouldering spots include Squamish, British Columbia, which has long been a staple destination on the great American summer road trip. Also, there is bouldering in the high Sierra peaks, the highest site being Mount Whitney, home to legendary alpine climbing but also to well-known bouldering areas such as Buttermilk Boulders.

Southern sandstone also affords excellent bouldering possibilities:

> Have you ever touched southern sandstone? If the answer is no, then you, my friend, are missing out in life. Picture this: You're in the woods, your crashpad is lying on a bed of golden leaves and soft dirt, the birds are chirping, it's 55°f and sunny, and before you lies a mega-classic, bubbly sandstone boulder, ready to be climbed. (Warnock, 2011, 44)

Thus, Warnock reveals that there are areas such as Rock Town in Georgia and Dayton Pocket, an hour or so north of Chattanooga, Tennessee, in the Laurel Snow State Natural Area, where there are many V6 and above boulder problems. (This is not an area for the fledgling boulderer, even though it is where the South's largest roof is to be found.) The South also boasts Horse Pens 40, Alabama, and Stone Fort, Chattanooga's largest bouldering area for face climbing. In addition, Hueco Tanks State

Historical Park, located 30 miles east of El Paso, Texas, is renowned for bouldering in winter, as summer days are usually too hot and also too dry for comfortable climbing.

> **Deep-water soloing, practiced on sea cliffs and at high tide, can also be done in the United States. Climbers do not have to go elsewhere to experience this style of climbing. (For instance, Thailand, Dorset in the United Kingdom, and Mallorca can offer excellent opportunities for this type of climbing.) However, not all of the deep-water soloing opportunities in the United States measure up to these global examples. Yet climbers can still head to the Alpine setting of Devil's Punch Bowl, Roaring Fork River, Independence Pass, in Colorado, where only 10 miles from Aspen is a pool with granite walls. Or climbers could visit Lake Travis, Pace Bend Park, Austin, Texas, for the limestone cliffs with very technical face climbing and overhanging jugs and tufas. Other deep-water soloing hot spots are to be found in Utah, Washington, and Squamish, British Columbia (Fox, 2011e).**

sport-climbing sites

In its 30-year history, sport climbing has undergone many changes. Sport climbing is defined as climbing on rock where predrilled bolts are already *in situ*. It was at Smith Rock State Park, Oregon, in the 1980s, that climbers such as Alan Watts, Bill Ramsey, and Chris Jones, aware that most of the aid climbs and cracks had been freed, looked anew at "the blank faces and stunning aretes that lay in between. Using the much controversial method of rap bolting and hangdogging, Watts created what were likely America's first sport climbs—Watts Tots (5.12b) and Chain Reaction (5.12c)—within a matter of weeks" (Siegrist, 2010, para. 2). Bolting routes as a new technique, with the bolts drilled onto the rock at intervals while rappelling, quickly took off all over the United States. (See Chapter 1, "Explanations," and Chapter 2, "Origins," for details of the debates that such ethics initially caused and for the arguments and passionate feelings bolting still causes.) In addition, the professional climber and writer Siegrist (2010) reveals that sport climbing continued to evolve throughout the mid-1990s, raising issues about the practice itself as well as hold manufacturing and even the concept of "pinkpoint" versus "redpoint." (*Redpoint* refers to leading a bolted route after inspection and possibly practicing moves on a toprope. Originally, if the quickdraws were placed prior to climbing, this was a pinkpoint. However, preplaced quickdraws became the norm and this is now known generally as a redpoint.)

This kind of climbing is now practiced on different types of rock in very diverse areas. As already noted in relation to the practice of bouldering, sport climbing areas go in and out of fashion. For example, Owen's River Gorge was the best sport-climbing site in California in the1980s. It then fell out of favor. Yet it is now fashionable once again. This is due in part to "its inexplicable roster of devotees, a veritable Who's Who of trad superstars" (Thornburg, 2009, 42). These "superstars" include the "trad icon" John Bachar. The result has been that the latest guidebook to the area has given the highest star rating to more than 50 routes.

In 1981, in the Las Vegas area, after a few years' worth of free climbs and aid routes having been put up, Lynn Hill and John Long, along with Joanne Urioste, freed "Levitation 29" (5.11c) in Red Rock Canyon. Then, in the late 1980s, Mike Tupper, Greg Mayer, and Don Welsh used rap-bolting to give Red Rock some of its first sport routes, enticing climbers such as Boone Speed and Bill Boyle from Salt Lake City for the winter climbing. Today, an area such as Red Rock Canyon, with its red and white sandstone, allows the climber to attempt multiple pitches, bouldering, and single-pitch sport climbing. Further, the areas around Las Vegas are drawing in climbers from the United States and around the globe. For example, these areas include Clark Mountain, with its limestone caves, where the hardest sport-climbing route in the United States to date is found; Mt. Charleston with its limestone crags; and Virgin River Gorge with hard sport limestone routes (Siegrist, 2011).

Another classic site for both sport climbing and bouldering is Joshua Tree, California, with its domes, pinnacles, and quartz monzonite boulders. Two new guidebooks to the Joshua Tree National Park area detail a staggering 8,000 climbs in the area. In the view of one of the authors of the guidebooks, the biggest change regarding any new sport routes being put up is how well a route is protected. New routes now have bolts placed every 6 to 10 feet as opposed to the many thousands of older routes, which often had 30-foot or greater runouts between the bolts. "Let your Freak Flag Fly" (5.7, 11 bolts) or "Piece of Cake" (513a, a short and powerful sport route) are recommended (MacDonald, 2011b). In comparison, an area such as St. George reveals that the bolting debate is alive and well in the Utah desert. Here, climbers speak about their bolting practices with passion and in terms of giving something back to the climbing community as well as allowing an intimate relationship with the rock itself (Mcinerney, 2011).

Meanwhile, at Red River Gorge, Kentucky, known for being the Southeast's most popular sport-climbing area, Sasha DiGiulian recently redpointed two 5.14c's: "Southern Smoke" and "Lucifer." She also on-sighted "Omaha Beach" (5.14a) and "Last of the Bohicans" (5.13d). At only 18 years of age, she is all the more remarkable as, worldwide, only a small number of women have climbed at this grade. Further, she is the first U.S. woman to on-sight 5.14a (Fox, 2011d). At Red Rocks, Nevada, the brilliant sport routes make the location a Californian hot spot for this kind of climbing. The Faulty Tower area is mostly shaded, the Great Wall of China has morning shade, while Pub Wall has afternoon shade. There is always top-class bouldering to be had at the Buttermilks; then, "when your skin starts to fail from the grainy rock, change direction and visit the less brutal Happys and Sads" (Fox, 2011f, 21).

But it is often not always accurate to see areas as consisting of only one type of climbing. For example, an area such as New River Gorge (West Virginia) has literally thousands of both sport and trad climbs. Moab, Utah, is infamous for sport and trad climbing on sandstone at Potash Road, as climbing journalist Fox (2011f) notes. Furthermore, in the Moab region, River Road has classic tower climbs, with Indian Creek for crack climbing being only one hour away to the south. Similarly, Chattanooga, Tennessee, and areas around it are a mecca for sport climbing, trad climbing, and bouldering.

traditional climbing sites

Trad climbing can be defined as climbing without bolts but with the need for the leader to place protection into gaps and cracks in the rock. This type of climbing incorporates big-wall climbing and mountaineering/alpine routes, for example. Classic areas for Alpine-style climbing include the high Sierra peaks, where Mount Whitney is the highest peak. For big-wall climbing, as was discussed in Chapter 1, it is true that Yosemite National Park splits into two places for rock climbing: "the Valley with its towering walls and crowded floor, and Tuolumne Meadows, a high and rolling expanse of lush forests punctuated by white and golden domes of rock" (Mellor, 2001, 210). Other classic regions for trad routes include the

Rocky Mountain National Park, Colorado, and well-known climbs there such as the east face of Long's Peak the "Diamond."

However, times change at such classic areas where climbing legends once were: "Visiting a Yosemite climbing camp today, you're just as likely to meet a divorce attorney from Delaware as a wild-haired dirtbag. Walking through Camp 4 one morning, I hear a dozen languages—Czech, Chinese, Thai, Italian—and meet climbers from all walks of life" (Jenkins, 2011, 110). Yet climbers such as Dean Potter, Ueli Steck, Alex Honnold, and Tommy Caldwell are still ensuring that Yosemite's spirit of adventure lives on, even if speed is now the ultimate challenge for today's climbers, rather than exploration, as was previously the case.

> **Since 2007, Caldwell has been busy free climbing a new route on El Cap, which is said to be possibly the world's hardest big-wall free climb in existence. As Caldwell recounts, "There's something magnetic about Yosemite. . . . All the history. I freak out the moment I get here and look up at the walls" (cited in Jenkins, 2011, 115). Furthermore, Alex Honnold claims that the limits for free soloing at Yosemite have not yet been fully tested.**

Elsewhere, another well-known area for trad climbing is Black Canyon at Gunnison National Park in Colorado. However, trad climbing takes place over the whole terrain of the United States and in lesser known places than Yosemite or Colorado. One current, if rather less well-known, trad climbing area is Devils' Lake State Park, Wisconsin, for Midwestern Utah-style crack climbing. In Zion National Park, Utah, there exist sandstone big walls and long routes that demand ultimate commitment, so that a portaledge may be needed for an overnight bivvy (emergency shelter) and long runouts are often to be expected (George, 2011). There is also high alpine adventure to be found in Utah's Lone Peak Cirque: "Though visible from all over greater Salt Lake City, the Cirque's tranquil splendour is only earned by a long, hot, steep, and dusty approach: five miles with more than 5,000 vertical feet of gain" (Burr, 2011, 57). This then leads to an arc of 400-foot solid granite walls.

Seneca Rocks, West Virginia, has face and crack climbing on multi-pitch trad routes. This area has been one of the great areas for trad climbing, from the heady days of the 1960s and 1970s, when top standard climbs for the day were established, to the 1980s and 1990s, when steep 5.11s to 5.13s were put up (Smith, 2010).

The Grand Tetons, in Wyoming, is a classic area where the "Exum Ridge" and "Owen Spalding" routes are rightly known for being popular alpine climbs, both due to their beauty and the fact they are two of the easiest ways to summit the iconic peak of the Grand Teton (Loomis, 2011). The area affords spectacular climbing for both the novice and the experienced climber alike despite snowfields and icy winds. However, Loomis (2011) also points out that there are over 90 other routes, which should not be forgotten if climbers want to avoid the crowds. For example, "Lower Exum Ridge" (III 5.7) and "Direct Petzoldt Ridge" (III 5.7) are just two of the excellent alternative routes.

In another region, the Cascades (which are in fact mostly extinct volcanoes, snow-topped and with rainforest and glaciers) afford mountaineering in the Pacific Northwest, running from northern California, with Mt. Shasta and Lassen Peak, north to Mt. Garibaldi in British Columbia. While the Cascades have served as a training ground for elite Alpine climbers, the mountaineering here is stupendous in its own right. The topography here has been described by the climbing journalist Connor (2011) as very varied, with routes on Mt. Hood being able to be done "car-car" and before lunch, if with a fast team, while others may take three days. In addition, "Some summits are so tiny that you're just, to quote a friend, 'one epileptic fit away from oblivion,' while others could, and have, housed an army encampment" (Connor, 2011, 65).

climbing competitions

All that is needed to climb indoors is a pair of climbing shoes, a harness, a belay device, and chalk, all of which can normally be hired. Some climbers rarely, if ever, venture away from the gym, seeing it as a form of exercise and a leisure pursuit in itself. Young children can also learn the elementary styles and techniques of climbing in a safe and supervised environment—for example, which knot to use to tie into the belay device, how to belay their partner safely, and so on. Also, some climbers build their own mini gyms at home, in a basement or garage, for instance, or train on a campus board. However, most gym users see indoor climbing as preparation for the "real thing." It is an environment where they can initially learn basic safety techniques or, later, train to getter better stamina or more endurance, for example, as preparation for climbing on real rock (see http://www.indoorclimbing.com).

It was in the 1970s that the first indoor climbing gyms (or walls, as they are called in the United Kingdom) emerged. They now exist all over the United States and more globally. Today's climbing gyms, through the advancement of climbing technology, can incorporate features such as moving walls, for instance, to make climbing an indoor route more difficult. Early indoor climbing venues were much simpler. Previously, the routes consisted of holds fashioned from wooden blocks nailed to a wall, often to simulate a route that would normally be found on the rock outside (see http://www.indoorclimbing.com).

Climbing competitions take place both indoors and outdoors on real rock. Moreover, today's climbing competitions have been seen to have two sources. One is that speed climbing grew out of an already institutionalized Soviet system of mountaineering in the period following World War II. The other is the French and, to a lesser degree, the Italian styles of rock climbing, which saw extreme speed climbing emerging from climbing on the boulders of Fontainebleau, near Paris, in the 1970s (Donnelly, 2003). The sport sociologist Donnelly also notes, however, that later,

> the route and its difficulty became rather more significant than the means of achieving it in the French style, and throughout the 1970s a style of climbing that involved bolting, hangdogging, hold-chipping (using a hammer to trim a razor edge and unusable flake of rock from into an edge broad enough to hold a climbing shoe), and other forms of route preparation began to develop. (Donnelly, 2003, 299)

Therefore, difficult and previously unclimbable routes could be attempted with a minimum of risk. At the same time, sponsorship of climbers by gear manufacturers, for example, also took hold.

Competition climbing gained popularity during the 1980s. The first sport-climbing competition took place in 1985 at Bardoneccia in Italy. Despite the increasing number of sport-climbing events around the world, it has been argued that competition climbing is not a good spectator sport:

> Competitors never face one another on the course. At the end of their turn, they simply untie from the rope and join their fellows at the edge of the crowd, the better to compare notes with those who have gone before—"How high did you get?"—commiserate with those who come after—"Tough one, dude. You were just a slap from the bucket"—and put away their gear while they watch and hope that the next guy out doesn't get as high on the wall as they did. (Dornian, 2003, 283)

However, Dornian also gives a number of reasons why indoor competition climbing is, for him, "the best sport in the world." For instance, he notes that it is not expensive, competitors are generally self-coached, and, though there are winners, there are also no losers. This is because the main aim is to perform well, and it is usually a competitor's overall ranking in a series that counts. Oh, and it's fun! These developments have not been without their detractors, however, who have argued that climbing's original maverick tendencies will become too sanitized and commercial due to competitive climbing, not to mention the red tape and control exerted by the organizing bodies that run these competitions.

The International Federation of Sport Climbing (IFSC) was founded in 2007. With 48 or more affiliated member federations and a headquarters in Turin, Italy, it remains the international governing organization for competition climbing. This includes the areas of bouldering, lead climbing, speed climbing, and youth competitions. Competition climbing in general tests the attributes of strength, ability, and technique, and often there is a monetary prize for the winners. In a bouldering event, competitors attempt a series of problems in as few tries as possible. Speed climbing is an attempt to get to the top of a route as quickly as possible. For lead or difficulty climbing, the competitor leads a bolted route, often on steep overhangs and using small holds that are put far apart (Oxlade, 2003).

There are also strict rules to such climbing competitions. Often, climbers have to climb the route in question on sight without seeing other climbers attempting the route. Nor can they get "beta," that is, advice on the route from other climbers, so they are held in isolation before a climb. Furthermore, usually, they only have a specific allotted time to inspect the route before they attempt it. Otherwise, this may give them an unfair advantage over other climbers in the same competition. Ice-climbing competitions, originating in Russia in the 1970s, have their own separate events, for example in speed and difficulty sections. The most well known in the United States is the Ouray Ice Festival, in Colorado, and this event attracts both competitors and gear manufacturers, having held its 16th meet in 2011.

Climbing competitions take place at local, regional, and national levels, with the latter two levels normally coming under the jurisdiction of the governing body. In addition, the IFSC and bouldering have made the short list for the 2020 Olympic Games. Further (and without a definitive empirical study!), indoorclimbing.com estimates that there are over 4,000 climbing walls (gyms) worldwide, with over 500 climbing competitions being held. Countries ranging from Argentina to Austria, Canada, China, the Czech Republic, Great Britain, Japan, Korea, Latvia, Norway, Pakistan, and the United States, for instance, all have their own regulating bodies.

Websites such as the U.S.-based 8a.nu (http://8a.nu) report on the competitions and also compile ranking tables for male and female climbers. These include sport and trad routes and boulder rankings on rock and rankings for junior climbers. For example, in relation to global performance on rock in a noncompetition sport-climbing setting, in September 2011 the Czech Adam Ondra led on the top 10 climbs in the last 12 months. Ondra also led in the boulder rankings, with U.S. climber Daniel Woods in second place. For female sport climbers in the same period using the same criteria, the American Sasha DiGiulian led, and the American Alex Puccio headed up the bouldering category. In the trad rankings for that period, Rogelio Pascual from Spain was number one, with American Alex Honnold close on his tail. The female trad rankings boasted two U.S. rock climbers, Katie Lambert and Elissa "Coaltrain" Williams in first and second place, respectively. There is often only a small overlap between those rock climbers who are successful in these rankings and in indoor competitions.

The popular X Games (summer and winter) consist of athletes from different sports, including skateboarding, BMX, and motocross in summer and skiing and snowboarding in winter, who meet in different cities worldwide to compete for prize money, medals, and peer recognition. In 2012, the summer X Games were held in Los Angeles. However, though rock climbing and ice climbing used to be included in the games, this is no longer the case, in large part due to the fact that climbing makes a poor spectator sport when televised globally.

Despite rock climbing no longer being part of the program for the X Games, climbing journalist Amanda Fox (2011i) notes that all three competitive types of climbing, which include boulder-ing, lead climbing, and speed climbing, are proposed for inclusion into the 2020 Olympic Games. Keith Ferguson, who was instrumental in creating the "Olympic Dream 2020 Bid Team," is currently trying to ensure that in 2013, when the final decision is taken regarding which new sports will be included, that climbing will not be dropped. Some, such as the president of the International Federation of Sport Climbing, Marco Maria Scolaris, take a positive stance on this potential inclusion. If successful, a wider audience will be able to appreciate the efforts of climbers as high-performing athletes. However, others take a more negative view, as being part of the games will both encourage competition and subject climbing to more rules and regulations, which could be seen to go against its nontraditional sporting past and image.

As detailed above, competitions test the speed, strength, and athletic ability of competitors, although as already indicated, there are different opinions in the climbing community on the benefits, or otherwise, of competition climbing. Such events bring climbing to the attention of a wider audience and provide some climbers with a living from prize money and sponsorship. However, increased involvement with organizations and sponsors can be seen to detract from climbing's image as an ethical and anticonsumer sport.

Yet, despite these different views, competition climbing goes from strength to strength. In a recent World Cup competition, Austria had wins at the Arco World Championships Lead Competition. The former world champions Angela Eiter of Austria and Ramón Julian Puigblanque of Spain finished in first place; Korean Jain Kim and Austrian Magdalena Röck were second and third, placing along with Austrian Jakob Schubert and Czech Adam Ondra. Sasha DiGiulian was the sole American to qualify for the finals, and she came in eighth (Fox, 2011b). In the IFSC Bouldering World Cup, held in Munich, Germany, in August 2011, the top three women climbers were from Slovenia, Germany, and Austria. Alex Puccio was the first female American to qualify in joint eighth position with Alizée Dufraisse from France. In the same competition, the top three men were from Russia, with Daniel Woods in 13th place, the first American male to make the grade (IFSC, 2011). Clearly, whether competition climbing is seen as a positive development or as further evidence of commercialization due to sponsorship of top climbers, it is a growing global aspect of the sport of rock climbing.

5. heroes

in an essay debating "What makes a climbing hero?" MacDonald (1999) explains that "It's more than just feats on rock and ice. To be a hero, a climber must somehow inspire other climbers, and everyone is inspired in different ways" (12). The climbing journalist adds that while we may be "inspired by legendary figures," it is ultimately "local heroes" that "make for great days out at the crags" (12).

Climbing, unlike most sports, is an activity where the greatest of climbers can literally be climbing on a route next to someone who only climbs on the weekend or at the lowest of grades. This is partly due to the physical location of climbs, so that hard routes exist side by side with less extreme ones, but also because climbing is a lifestyle sport that encourages crossover between different groups and kinds of climbers at the campsite, the bar, or at indoor gyms. As one climber wrote in a letter to *Rock and Ice* magazine,

> It says much about our sport that a lowly climber like me has bumped into and even climbed with such legends as Randy Leavitt, Bob Kamps, Jim Bridwell, Ron Kauk and others. . . . I will never forget John Bachar ripping through Camp 4 in a golf cart holding a bottle of whiskey in one upraised hand, howling to the moon and at the devil. I remember climbing at Tahquitz and feeling like I was on sacred ground, for all the history and famous climbers that had come before me. These ghosts are still a source of pride and inspiration. . . . (Barlow, 2009, 17)

However, as with any other sport, the ability to climb harder or faster, to be stronger or have more stamina, grit, determination, and focus, means that some sportsmen and women become elevated above others. As another climber and writer states,

Ron Kauk climbing the Killer Pillar at Yosemite National Park in Yosemite, California. (Mike Powell /Allsport/Getty Images)

> The strongest ties we have in climbing are our myths: the fables spun from parking lot to bar, from one crag to another, from climber to climber until the details are so convoluted and confused that all that remains is the telling. The written word can't capture what it really means to climb. The things that happen on rock are simply too visceral, too complex and personal to lay down on a page. The best climbing stories are the ones told out loud. (Childs, 1998, 74)

And so climbing legends are made from tales passed down over generations, in a oral sporting tradition, for instance in bars and around the campfire but also through interviews and personal accounts of climbing published in the climbing press, climbing writing and autobiographies, and, more recently, through film, the Internet, blogs, and forums. Regardless of the source, some stories take on a life of their own, and not all narratives are free from self-promotion, exaggeration, and sometimes downright lies!

Both elite climbing legends and non-elite climbers are profiled in a variety of media. These include climbing magazines that feature famous climbers, offer advice on training and injuries, and serve as a forum for climbers to access information about climbing hot spots, for instance. Currently in the United States, the main national climbing magazines that are available are *Rock and Ice*, *Climbing*, and *Urban Climber*. All of these publications are available in hard copy and in digital form, and the magazines have their own websites for the wider climbing community. (The climbing magazine *Alpinist* ceased publishing in 2008 due to the financial downturn at the time.) Online publications, websites (for example, those representing gear manufacturers or individual climbers), and blogs, as well as specialist forums, are also available to provide support, advice, and inspiration for interested climbers at whatever level they are involved in the sport. For instance, the website 8a.nu gives updated U.S. and world rankings for different types of climbing. Famous climbers such as Chris Sharma, Sasha DiGiulian, and Daniel Woods have their own websites and blogs where they relay to other climbers what their achievements have been or what is currently on their wish list to climb. Thus, even though some climbers choose not to be part of the climbing "scene," climbing is now a virtual, as well as an actual, community.

Climbing has also been the subject of films, where Hollywood heroes such as Sylvester Stallone have played climbers in adventure films such as *Cliffhanger* (1993). However, climbers represent themselves and their sport in less mainstream ways and often make their own films and videos. These are then screened at film festivals or on the annual Reel Rock Film Tour, for example, which shows climbing and adventure films in over 200 cities across the globe. Festivals such as the Banff Mountain Film and Book Festival held in Canada, or the Kendal Mountain Festival in the United Kingdom, celebrate the best of the literature and films of the climbing world.

Aron Ralston, recently portrayed in 2010 in the film *127 Hours*, reveals how the extraordinary and risk aspects of the alternative sport of rock climbing can engage the general public enough to inspire a best-selling and generally well-regarded film. In the film, he cuts off his own arm with a penknife in order to survive when climbing in Utah canyons after a dislodged boulder fell on his right arm:

My hand has almost jellified. The knife tip goes in and "pssstt," the gases from decomposition escape and there's this putrid smell. I go into this rage. I'm in this hyper-emotional state after all this regimented discipline to keep it all together and in this moment, when I'm trying to rip my arm out from the rock, I feel it bend and it stops me—"That's it! I can use the boulder to break my bones!" (Cited in Barkham, 2010, 8)

More alternative films to those mainstream offerings, such as
127 Hours, are produced by smaller companies, for example,
Sender Films and Big UP Productions. These are then screened
to smaller numbers of people than Hollywood audiences but
aim, as the publicity for the Reel Rock Film Tour 2011 states, to
provide

> a mind-blowing, palm-sweating pump-fest of climbing flicks for
> the 6th annual REEL ROCK Film Tour. We've gathered the
> wildest climbing stories from around the globe: The legendary
> race for The Nose speed record; The queen of the of-width
> cracks; A nine year old bouldering prodigy; Tommy Caldwell's
> efforts on the hardest big wall free climb; A crazed high-lining
> champion; And the most insane ice climbing action ever and
> more. It's all part of the cinematic tour de force that is REEL
> ROCK VI. (Reel Rock Tour, 2011, para.1)

The British sociologist Barry Smart (2005) points out that after World
War I, there was a high level of hero worship in the United States, sug-
gesting that this occurred because of the new media of popular culture
such as mass-circulation magazines, radio, and television, but also
because people craved escape from the war years. Heroic figures were
invested with virtue and allowed people respite from economic and technological change. At the same time, organized sport took on a new cultural significance. Smart also charts the move after World War II from
the "effortless grace" of a past, gentler heroism, to a world of sport that
is now professional, competitive, and often motivated by financial reward.
Further, heroism can have national imperialistic overtones, as the U.S.
academic Bayers (2003) argues in relation to mountaineering and British
and American imperialism. This can be seen from Victorian times up to
the present, with the contemporary example of "would be mountaineers"
who pay to be guided up Everest, when sometimes local Sherpa guides
die helping these paying clients to summit.

Today's climbers the world over are now a part of this changing
dynamic as extreme sports cross over into the mainstream, and heroes
great and small earn their reputations in this rapidly changing sporting

Actor Sylvester Stallone in a scene from the 1993 film *Cliffhanger.* (Tri-Star/
Photofest)

world. How the great climbing heroes of the past contrast to those young
climbers who grace the pages of the climbing media, or who are the subject of admiration on rock-climbing forums such as 8a.nu, is an interesting
topic. Some compare the rock gods who strolled around Camp 4 at

Yosemite in the 1960s and 1970s, bedecked in hippie garb, to the media-savvy, self-promoting career climbers of today. They often lament the loss of the former, who were untainted by the commercialization that could be said to characterize modern climbing. But it can equally be argued that such classifications are too simplistic, and each era has its own heroes who inspire others to take to the rock, as well as unique forms of communication that help these stories travel across the climbing culture.

Contemporary climbing heroes, therefore, do not escape this new brash commercial world, but rather are increasingly becoming a part of it. Yet some climbers, even when sponsored or professional, through force of personality or sheer talent coupled with charisma, still manage to tread a fine line between commercial sell-out and heroic endeavor. In the United States, these currently include male climber Chris Sharma and female climbers Alex Puccio and Sasha DiGiulian. These sportsmen and -women continue to have purchase on the climbing community's popular imagination and remain inspirational to their climbing peers.

Constructing a comprehensive list of the most influential and inspirational climbers in the United States is a difficult task. Any list inevitably risks leaving worthy people out, and such a list is subject to who is popular now, and who might not be so in years to come. The following list is by no means a definitive one. Rather, the climbers have been selected to reveal the different styles and types of climbing (i.e., aid climbing, free climbing, big-wall climbing, sport climbing, and bouldering) from different periods. The selected climbers include early pioneers as well as some of today's hot shots. Male and female climbers are profiled, yet there are fewer women featured due to the fact that it was not until the late 1970s and 1980s that women really started to push the grades and gain a more national, and in some cases international, reputation. This was due partly to the global rise of feminism and the women's movement, which encouraged women to compete on the same terms as men across a number of spheres, including sport.

The list focuses on rock climbing; thus, mountaineers such as Reinhold Messner or Conrad Anker are excluded here. Most climbers are from the United States, with mention of others from different countries, particularly the United Kingdom, given the influence UK climbers have had on the U.S. climbing scene. Other key climbers not specifically mentioned here are acknowledged for their contributions to the sport and lifestyle in other chapters in this book. Further, any such list of influential climbers might start with the name of the Scottish-born author, naturalist, and conservationist John Muir (1838–1894). In Chapter 2, "Origins," it was argued that the early roots of climbing could be traced back to 1869 with Muir's free climbing of Cathedral Peak in the High Sierra above Yosemite Valley. Further, as befits the history of a country such as the United States with its rich history of immigration, the first climber of note here originally hailed from Germany.

people, places, and achievements

fritz weissner (1900–1988)

Weissner was born in Germany but emigrated to the United States in 1929 at the age of 29. He became known as a pioneer of free climbing, for his skills in wide-crack climbing, and as the climber who developed the Shawangunks and routes in New Hampshire's White Mountains. It was Weissner who did two of North America's "last great problems": Devils Tower, Wyoming, and Mt. Waddington, British Columbia (Webster, 1999). In fact, before the Californians could take the prize of Mt. Waddington in the 1930s, Weissner "bagged" the climb. Describing the experience, he recalls, "Mentally and physically I was keyed up to the very high pitch which one reaches on certain occasions: at this time I knew that the summit would be ours. Determined, and feeling that no obstacle of a technical nature could stop us, I started on the rocks" (cited in Jones, 1997, 157). As climbing author Jones (1997) further recounts, it was Weissner who had precisely the right qualities to climb the mountain, having led climbs on sandstone towers in Dresden, Germany, that were possibly the hardest in Europe at the time. In addition, he was a leading German mountaineer, giving him a technical and psychological edge over his U.S. climbing rivals.

Weissner awed many of his climbing contemporaries with his view that if it was important enough, a first ascent was worth risking life for. In 1935, along with a close friend, Hans Krauss, he initiated climbing at the Shawangunks' "Skytop" cliffs. His lead climbing of "The Gargoyle" there showed his great technical skills, vision, and physical strength but also that even very steep climbs could be surmounted at a good standard of technical difficulty (Waterman and Waterman, 1993). Climbing until the age of 86, this was "the man who, in deference to his Sherpa partner's request, turned back only 800 feet shy of the summit of K2 in 1939" (Webster, 1999, 78). Clearly, such a calculated approach to risk enabled him to live a long life filled with many climbing feats.

royal robbins (1935–)

Robbins, born in West Virginia, 35 years after Weissner, was particularly known for his pioneering and technical aid exploits on Yosemite's granite walls in the 1960s. His incredible list of first ascents on Yosemite's big walls include the notable 1957 ascent of the northwest Face of Half Dome, with Mike Sherrick and Jerry Gallwas, which was the first grade-VI climb in the United States. In 1961, with Tom Frost and Chuck Pratt, his "Salathé Wall," El Capitan, was then the hardest big-wall grade-VI climb in the world. In 1963, he was the first climber to solo a big aid route at Yosemite when he climbed "Leaning Tower" in awful weather conditions, and in 1968, in 10 days, he made the first solo of El Capitan on the "Muir Wall" route. In 1998, during a trip to Great Britain, he was influenced by the British climbers Joe Brown and Don Whillans and became intrigued by the British use of "climbing nuts" as protection. Upon his return to the United States, he continued to advocate the use of climbing bolts, which he saw as not damaging the rock as well as being easy to use.

The writer and climber Pat Ament (1999) (of some repute himself, being known for first ascents at Yosemite and Colorado in the 1960s and 1970s) describes Robbins's ideas on climbing in the 1960s as being both "severe" and "pure," though sometimes he was misunderstood, given his definite views on climbing issues. In two influential books, *Basic Rockcraft* and *Advanced Rockcraft*, Robbins passionately advocated free-climbing skills and a clean-climbing ethic. He has been described as one of the United States' most celebrated climbers:

> In a world that respects its heroes and holds them in highest esteem, the name Royal Robbins is hallowed. There are after all, few climbers so accomplished, who have such a record of achievement and whose values transcend all ethical debate to the point where his ideals formed the very basis of style during a golden era of climbing history and still do, to this day. (Shepherd, 1998, 39)

He also founded an outdoor clothing business with his wife, Liz Robbins, and though eventually he had to give up climbing due to arthritis, the adventure sport of kayaking still gave him a connection to the great outdoors.

> **Robbins described himself as "like Walt Whitman," that is "a mixture of sublimity and garbage—well not quite like the Good Grey Poet, and certainly not sublime" (Robbins, 2002, 63).**

john gill (1937–)

Representative of another style of climbing entirely different from Robbins's, and born only two years after, Gill is known to many in the United States and the rest of the world as the founder of American bouldering and for applying gymnastic techniques (and gymnastic chalk) to rock climbing. His strength was also well known through his one-finger pull-ups. Between 1955 and the mid-1970s, "he left mini-masterpieces at major rock climbing areas throughout America" (Achey, Chelton, & Godfrey, 2002, 70). Of bouldering as a style of climbing, he himself said, "In spirit, bouldering is the quintessential kinesthetic experience in rock climbing. It is the soul of rock climbing: the fascinating acrobatic synthesis of man and rock" (cited in Achey, Chelton, & Godfrey, 2002, 70). However, as an early pioneer, Ament (1992) notes that he was shunned in the late 1950s and early 1960s because his climbing was centered around small boulders or more obscure solo climbs in the Tetons. But in doing these boulder problems, he most likely devised the first grading system for bouldering (the B1 system), which was applicable to bouldering routes in different areas: "His achievements have been battles in wit that deepen, upon reflection, to subtle espousals of philosophy. Critical to that philosophy has been a strong appreciation of nature: sky, streams, wildlife, differing colors of the rock, hills delicately in bloom, and the forests and air" (Ament, 1992, 1). Given the current popularity of bouldering in the United States and worldwide, his influence cannot be overestimated.

yvon chouinard (1938–)

A contemporary of Royal Robbins, Yvon Chouinard was renowned for both his big-wall climbing in Yosemite in the "Golden Age" of the 1960s (with Robbins, Chuck Pratt, and Tom Frost) and for his innovations in climbing equipment. A particularly notable climb of Chouinard's, along with Robbins, Pratt, and Frost, was his first ascent of "North America Wall," El Capitan, in 1964. Before that, with Pratt and Warren Harding, he climbed the 2,800-foot south face on Mt. Watkins in Yosemite Valley in dreadfully hot conditions. In 1965, with T.M. Herbert, he made the first ascent of "Muir Wall," El Capitan (VI 5.10 A3). Of the groundbreaking El Cap ascent, in which they had not used fixed ropes, he said, "No longer would we ever be afraid of spending so many days on a climb, whether it was a Yosemite wall or a long Alaskan ridge" (cited in Arce, 1996, 67). Furthermore, his transferring

Patagonia climbing and gear company owner and noted climber Yvon Chouinard. (Getty Images)

of big-wall climbing techniques to mountain climbing ensured his historical contribution to alpinism in Europe and also Pakistan. Chouinard was also well known among his peers for his creativity in designing rock-climbing equipment. His legendary chrome-moly-steel pitons, for example, revolutionized how the cracks at Boulder, Colorado, were to be climbed. In 1972, after a successful career as a climber and many years of technological innovation, Chouinard went on to found the very successful worldwide Patagonia outdoor clothing company.

layton kor (1938–)

Born in the same era as both Robbins and Chouinard, Kor is culturally renowned for his climbing achievements in Colorado during the 1960s.

> **Pat Ament recalls getting a phone call from the climber Layton Kor in 1962: "Ament, you gotta get down here right away. Bring all the money you can get hold of. There's somebody here selling Chouinard equipment. It's incredible" (cited in Achey, Chelton, & Godfrey, 2002, 35).**

As one climbing journalist writes, "Wearing hard-soled boots and a swami belt, with a dreadfully heavy rack of pitons, stiff goldline rope and no sponsors, Layton Kor put up an unbelieveable number of classic routes" (Luebben, 1999, 72). Kor teamed up with the climber Bob Culp, who at the time was labeled Colorado's number two climber, and the pair started to solo routes there in earnest; despite Kor being in bad health due to the lung fungus San Joaquin Valley fever, he regained strength. In 1961, both of them climbed desperate routes in such as the 1,500-foot, 5.9-grade northwest face of Chiefshead in Rocky Mountain National Park. Kor later went on to make the early ascents of climbs such as "Spider Rock," "Cleopatra's Needle," and the "Totem Pole," which had been pioneered by climbers from Southern California (Jones, 1997). And, on the rock walls around Boulder, Kor "was probably the best all-round rock climber in the country in his ability to get up any given piece of rock" (Jones, 1997, 274–75).

Such climbing genius does not, however, always make for an easy-going character. Kor was aware of both the value and joy of life but could be impatient with his climbing partners, who were often physically weaker: "Kor sometimes simply pulled his partner up if the person took too long. The unreasonableness of it all!" (Ament, 2002b, 102). And it was true that Kor went through partners in double-quick time. On climbing "Jack of Diamonds" on Longs Peak, Colorado, in 1963, with the great climber Robbins, Robbins said of the climb, "I was at the height of my climbing powers and quite fit. I kept pace with Kor, but only by extending myself to the utmost, and I was keeping pace with him rather than the other way around" (Luebben, 1999, 72). After climbing many significant routes in Colorado, Utah, Yosemite, Canada, and the Dolomites, Kor ceased climbing in the late 1960s when he became a Jehovah's Witness. But his reputation continues: "When Layton Kor, age 70 and seriously ill with kidney disease, agreed to a slide show at Neptune Mountaineering, in Boulder, the presentation sold out in nine minutes ... 'One word: iconic,' said Jim Donini—recent president of the American Alpine Club" (cited in Osius, 2009a, 24).

jim bridwell (1944–)

Jim Bridwell had arguably the widest vision and greatest influence of all the Yosemite climbers. He has been described as a trendsetter for over 25 years; leading on the first-ever one-day ascent of El Capitan in 1975

> **Bridwell's photo, along with John Long and Billy Westbay, caught on camera as colorful hippies after their successful ascent of "The Nose" in 1975, with El Capitan as their backdrop, "etched in the collective mind that American climbers were surly and irreverent, at a station confidently distinct from their European contemporaries" (Mellor, 2001, 217). His climbing companion Long said of the climb, "Smiling at the great rock, Bridwell blew out a cloud of Camel smoke and said, 'Boys, we'll all do harder things. But a first like this can only be done once, and we'll never top it' " (cited in Huber and Zak, 2003, 109).**

(done in 15 hours). He is infamous for being masterful at aid climbing and for climbing in the Alps and Alaska as well as the continental United States. He also became a symbol of U.S. rock climbing recognized by climbers around the world (Mellor, 2001). Whether he was worshipped, loathed, or loved, Bridwell's exploits over the years are legendary. The climbing writer Geoffrey Childs recounts, "Relying on pitons hand-forged by Yvon Chouinard in the Camp 4 parking lot and Austrian kletterschues, Bridwell and his cohorts practiced a ground-up ethic that outlawed previewing, hangdogging, or resting on gear" (Childs, 1998, 79). With such a legacy, he can be seen to have played a major role in defining climbing as we know it today. Yet he is, reportedly, uncomfortable with all the fuss that surrounds his climbing exploits. As the climber John Long said, "Americans are tough on their heroes. . . . The things that made him so good as a climber make him a pretty easy target for people who don't really know him. I know it bothers him, but his answer has always been to go put up another route. To let his climbing speak for him" (cited in Childs, 1998, 151). More recently, since 2001, his continuing influence on today's younger generation of climbers was shown in his advising of the UK climber Leo Houlding on climbing the southeast face of El Capitan.

john bachar (1957–2009)

Bachar hailed from Southern California and began climbing in his early teens on sandstone at Stoney Point, north of Los Angeles (where Yosemite climbers such as Robbins, Chouinard, and Herbert would also train at various times). At Yosemite, he formed a deep friendship with fellow climber Ron Kauk, and by the late 1970s they were certainly two of the best climbers in the United States (Arce, 1996). With many free ascents behind them both, including "Astro Man" (5.11d) and the first free ascent of "Hotline" (512a), being one of the first at that grade in Yosemite, they went on to be known worldwide for their free-climbing achievements. In 1981, with Dave Yerian, another climber and his good friend, he had on-sighted the famous "Bachar-Yerian" (5.11c R) on Mendlicott Dome in Tuolumne Meadows, California. As climbers Huber and Zak (2003) acknowledge, Bachar opted to climb routes in the traditional manner, while Kauk rap-bolted routes such as "European Vacation" (5.13b). However, Bachar was seduced by free soloing in particular.

Bachar was also known for his legendary fitness and training regimes (designing an overhanging rope ladder named the Bachar ladder) and for the injuries he sustained during training: "Some of what we know now about how not to over-train comes from John's eagerness for preparation, probing the outer limits of fitness" (Robinson, 2009, 58). He infamously offered $10,000 to anyone who could follow him soloing for a day. No one did. Climbing writer Daniel Duane (1999) compares his one-bolt routes to performance art and as being an antithesis to the conservatism of sport climbing in the 1980s, when endless bolts on climbs at Tuolumne Meadows were the norm. With such ethical purity came controversy and arguments, even rage, with other climbers who disagreed with him. However, "He was just the guy who did what you could never, ever do—who did what none of the climbers who called themselves 'the best' could ever, ever do—and he was the guy who did it more or less quietly" (76). In 2009, he died in a free solo accident at Dike Wall near Mammoth Lakes, California. Climbing journalist Raleigh (2009a) felt that he had "generated enough ink" (56) over 30 years of a climbing career to rival even someone as famous as Sir Edmund Hillary, and doubts his status will ever be equaled within the rock-climbing culture.

john sherman (1959–)

Of the same generation as Bachar, Sherman has been identified as one of the United States' best-known and skilled boulderers: "Probably no one has visited so many of America's legendary bouldering areas or so many of its good but obscure bouldering locations" (Ament, 2002c-, 8). Sherman himself wrote about the history and characters who took bouldering to new heights in the United States in his book *Stone Crusade: A*

Historical Guide to Bouldering in America, published in 1994. In the book, he answers those who criticize bouldering for not being a legitimate climbing activity by stating, "Our sport is the most analytical and perhaps the most physically demanding of all climbing activities, focusing almost exclusively on the underlying essence of modern climbing technical difficulty" (1994, xvii). In 1980, Sherman put up "Germ Free Adolescence" in Eldorado Canyon. He has also developed the Hueco Tanks area, and he is seen to have initiated the modern V scale for grading bouldering problems. The first line of his book *Sherman Exposed* (1999) reads, "On my van is a bumper sticker that reads 'Sport Climbing is Neither' " (9). This stance is testament to the traditional, antibolting position he held in the later 1980s and 1990s.

lynn hill (1961–)

While many women have made valuable contributions to climbing over the years, Hill was in a league of her own, such that *Rock and Ice* magazine described her as the "greatest rock climber in the world" on September 20, 1994 (1999, 78). This statement was based on exploits such as her being the first woman to climb 5.14, a long list of first free ascents, and, the jewel in her crown, her one-day free ascent in 1993 of "The Nose," the 3,000-foot route on El Capitan in Yosemite. It was, indisputably, an amazing display of technical skill and stamina. As Huber and Zak (2003) state regarding her freeing "The Nose," "Her words of 'It goes, boys!' were provocative but true" (139). And they offer as further evidence of this Hill's later redpointing of all the pitches, in 1994, on "The Nose" in 23 hours. Both her exploits on "The Nose" were not repeated for over 10 years, a staggering feat for a climber of either sex. This made her, at the time, the most accomplished female climber the world had ever known.

She describes climbing as always "challenging": "I'm constantly reaching down within myself to find a way to do something. Even if you don't succeed, it's still a good lesson, and in fact, that's usually when I learn the most. I think it's the greatest sport in the world" (cited in Greene, 1998, 48). Dubbing her the "ultimate rock chick," climbing author Douglas (2002) thinks that rock climbing appeals to Hill because it brings together different elements such as ambition, a love of the outdoors, athleticism, and, something many American climbers of her generation embrace, a rebellious counterculture. At present, Hill still climbs and is currently a sponsored athlete for the Patagonia gear and clothing company.

> **In Lynn Hill's autobiography *Climbing Free*, she recalls her attempt to climb "The Nose" in under 24 hours:**
>
> I found myself below the last two pitches at nightfall. . . . At the final bulge I was so drained of strength that I had to leap for a hold in a hit-or-miss style. The battery in my torch was fading almost as quickly as the strength in my arms. But I arrived at the summit, after 23 hours of climbing. It has taken years for me fully to digest what took place that day. (cited in Douglas, 2002, 44)

robyn erbesfield-raboutou (1963–)

Born just two years after Hill, Erbesfield-Raboutou did the first 5.13c on-sight by a woman in 1993, the same year she became the third woman to climb 5.14 (Lynn Hill was the first). In addition, she has won four World Cup titles in the 1990s for sport climbing. And, at the age of 45, "Fifteen years ago Robyn Erbesfield-Raboutou was the third woman to climb 5.14. Now she's just completed another 5.14a (8b+) near her summer home in France. Erbesfield-Raboutou redpointed *Bad Attitude*, a route established many years ago by her husband, Didier, at St. Antonin Noble Val" (MacDonald, 2008, para. 1). Flashing 5,13a, and V9, she now climbs with her family. When asked recently what her climbing goals currently are, she stressed that she wants to continue to be strong but also wants to build the next generation of world champion youth climbers (Erbesfield-Raboutou, 2011). In 2011, she sent her first V11 boulder problem with "Hard Boiled" in Boulder Canyon, Colorado, which she had worked on with her son Shawn, age 12. Shawn had recently sent his first V11, with Schwerer Gustov, at Hueco Tanks, Texas (dpm, 2011).

dean potter (1972–)

Dean Potter is well known for having speed-soloed Half Dome, El Capitan, Cerro Torre, and Fitzroy, as well as for being the first climber to make a one-day free ascent of El Capitan and Half Dome. He is also famous for a one-day speed linkup of both of those big walls and Mount Watkins, Yosemite's third Grade VI wall. In addition to these achievements, he has walked highlines without a safety leash and recently has combined his BASE jumping skills with both highlining and free soloing, using a specially engineered BASE rig, which is ultralight, as backup (prAna, 2011). In sum, as well as being an alpinist, he is known for doing hard first ascents, free solo ascents, speed ascents, and enchainments (climbing two or more routes in a single outing), particularly in Yosemite, but also in Patagonia. He has been referred to as the "Dark Wizard" who experimented with "the dark arts—things like free soloing" where risk is at its utmost (Bisharat, 2010d, para. 6). He has also courted controversy for doing unauthorized climbs such as "Delicate Arch" in Arches National Park, Utah, losing sponsorship in the process. In 2010, he said, "Soloing for me is about being completely in the moment, not worrying about the past or future, but just being right here, right now. That's why I do it" (Climb and More.com, 2007, para. 1).

lisa rands (1975–)

A sponsored, professional climber, Rands was born in 1975 and is particularly known for her competition climbing and bouldering in the United States and for climbing on gritstone in the United Kingdom's Peak District. She became the first American to win an international bouldering World Cup. Despite her many successes in both indoor and outdoor competitions, Rands prefers the latter because, in her own words, "I grew up climbing on real rock" so "those types of competitions are always my favorite" (SCC, 2010, para. 10).

Rands is also a renowned boulderer. In 2008, she did the famous "The Mandala" (V12), which made her the first woman to do so since Chris Sharma climbed it previously. Rands is also known for her success on hard, very risky traditional routes in the United Kingdom's Peak District, including ascents of "The End of the Affair" at Curbar Edge in 2004 and also "Gaia" at Black Rocks in 2006. Both were E8s. "Gaia" was later flashed for the first time by fellow American Alex Honnold in 2008.

Such climbs made her the first woman ever to lead a grit E8 route and in so doing ensured she was a role model for future generations of female climbers.

tommy caldwell (1978–)

Born in 1978, Caldwell is widely regarded as "America's best all-round rock climber": "the product of an enthusiastic father, natural talent, and raw desire, Caldwell embodies the potential of a new generation of climbers" (Kroese, 2001, 49). Before the age of 21, he was already the first

> Of his climbing, Tommy said, "I pretty much get to pick where I want to go and climb full-time. It's awesome. I can't imagine a better life" (cited in Kroese, 2001, 49).

American to lead all the pitches on "Salathé Wall" in Yosemite and put up the one of the United States' hardest sport climbs at the time, in Colorado, "Kryptonite" (5.14d). Caldwell free and speed climbs on big walls and sport climbs, and he has first free and free ascents of a number of El Capitan routes under his belt. In May 2004, he achieved the first free ascent of "Dihedral Wall." One year later, with Beth Rodden, he made the third and fourth free ascents of "The Nose," and a mere two days after, he free climbed "The Nose" in less than 12 hours. Literally a few days after this feat, he then ascended "The Nose" in 11 hours, descended the "East Ledges," and then went up "Freerider," topping out 12 hours later. This was, therefore, effectively the first ascent of two El Capitan free climbs done within 24 hours. In an accident in 2001, Caldwell sawed off much of his left index finger. Doctors reattached the digit, but Caldwell later had it removed so as not to hold up his progress—such is his dedication to the sport. Together, in 2010, Caldwell and Kevin Jorgeson started the fourth year of their attempt to free climb El Capitan's tallest and smoothest sector, "Dawn Wall," in Yosemite, which is argued to be the world's hardest rock climb. Bad storms made them abandon this latest attempt.

leo houlding (1980–)

Houlding is the latest in a long line of distinguished British climbers. This includes Joe Brown, who was one of the world's leading climbers in the 1950s and 1960s after pioneering climbs of Snowdonia and the Peak District in the United Kingdom and the Himalayas.

According to British mountaineer Sir Chris Bonington, "Leo is bold, innovative, energetic, inspirational and most important of all, fun to be around. He has become very much the ambassador for the younger generation of climbers" (cited on http://www.leohoulding.com). In his early 30s, Houlding remains one of the best climbers in Britain and, indeed, the world. As his personal website states, his speciality is free climbing some of the most technical peaks, including Everest, and the biggest walls in the world. He has also made his mark in para-alpinism (climbing up, then flying down).

Other British climbers of repute have included Pete Livesey,
who was internationally known in the 1970s for putting up hard
routes and training professionally; and Ron Fawcett, known for
climbing hard, traditional routes in the 1970s and early 1980s.
The British climber Stevie Haston said of Fawcett, "We had had
professional mountaineers before but not a rock climbing professional. Ron paved the way for the Sharmas of the future"
(Haston, 2010, para. 4). In the 1980s and 1990s, the British
Jerry Moffatt climbed at Yosemite, Joshua Tree, and Colorado,
putting up first ascents and lightning-quick repeats of local
test pieces, earning him a place in a recent list of the top 25
influential climbers in the American publication *Rock and Ice*
(Jackson, 2009b).

In the United States, Houlding is best known for his audacious efforts
(since 2001) to eventually free a new route on El Capitan, which was from
the ground up and with no bolts or portaledge. As referred to earlier,
Houlding had worked the route previously with Jason Pickles and used
the advice of American veteran climber Bridwell in his attempt.
Climbing editor Jackson (2011a) sees this feat as inspirational, and so he
urges the more ordinary climber, "you may feel like you, too, can try a little harder, run it out between placements, maybe go for it instead of back-
ing down" (8). Houlding has been sponsored by outdoor manufacturer
Berghaus for over 13 years.

beth rodden (1980–)

Originally from California, Rodden began climbing at a young age and
had many early successes in climbing competitions, winning the Junior
National JCCA Championships in 1996, 1997, and 1998. She was ranked
first overall in the ASCF adult national series in 1997 and 1998 and also
placed third at the ASCF Fall Nationals in 1998. Despite her successes as
a competition climber, she is particularly well known for her trad climbing skills. She was the youngest woman to climb 5.14a and places herself
in the contemporary climbing scene, where she is a sponsored, professional climber, thus: "I was part of the so-called 'first generation of kid
climbers,' which included Chris Sharma, Tommy Caldwell and Katie
Brown, among others. Looking back, that was an exciting time. There

weren't that many of us. We were just going for it" (Rodden, 2009, para. 1). She is an exceptionally talented climber, with previous ascents up to 5.14b/F8c ("The Optimist," first ascent) and free ascents of "The Nose," "Lurking Fear," and "El Corazon" on the legendary El Capitan (Geldard, 2008). When she climbed "Meltdown" in 2008, it made her one of the world's top traditional climbers on one of the hardest trad routes at the time. Of "Meltdown," she said, "5.14 is freakin' hard. *Meltdown* [5.14c trad climb, FA, Yosemite] was not just trying physically, but mentally because it took me over 40 days—absolutely the longest I've ever spent on a single route" (Rodden, 2009, para. 10). She married but later divorced fellow climber Caldwell. Climbing recently has been difficult for her due to injuries sustained over the last few years. But she is still considered by many to be hugely influential on the current scene.

chris sharma (1981–)

Sharma is widely recognized as one of the most progressive contemporary climbers:

> Picking projects at your physical and mental limits means constant exposure to the reality of failure. The struggle crushes many, weeding out the strong-fingered charlatans from the lifers. Above it all reigns Chris Sharma, 26, an athlete endowed with unparalleled physical strength and mental tenacity, dominating world sport climbing and bouldering for the last dozen years. (Cahall, 2010, para. 2)

Sharma was only 14 years old when he won the US Bouldering Nationals, and at the age of 15 he did a 5.14c, which in that period was the hardest climb rating in the U.S. grading system. As climbing journalist Lowell (1999) details, he also has won international competitions without training, done 5.13 climbs while wearing clogs on his feet, and done V8s and V9s in sneakers and flip-flops:

> The idea of climbing something "important," something to impress the world, means nothing to Chris. In that regard, those who feel he doesn't take climbing seriously are correct. When he reflects on climbing in the context of the universe, he sees it as ultimately insignificant. "It's a hobby," he says. "Climbing's climbing. It's supposed to be fun. If it's not fun, why do it?" (1999, 90)

Despite this relatively carefree attitude, he has completed many famous climbs including "Realization" (5.15a) at Ceüse, France, in 2001; red-pointing "Jumbo Love," a 250-foot climb at Clark Mountain, California, in 2008; and also "Golpe de Estado," another 5.15b in Siurana, Spain. In relation to the latter, he said, "I think this area of Spain has undoubtedly become the epicenter of global sport climbing" (cited in Bisharat, 2009b, 16). In 2008, he won the Mammut bouldering championships in Salt Lake City, Utah, being the only finalist in the competition to flash three problems. In 2011, only two weeks after he completed the infamous "First Round First Minute" project in Margalef, Spain, he then climbed a 5.15b and 5.15a at Oliana in the same day.

daniel woods (1989–)

Woods is currently one of the world's leading boulderers. He started climbing at the age of 5, in Texas, and his passion and commitment to the sport are already legendary despite his young age. He therefore serves as an inspiration to the new, younger generation of climbers. He is sponsored by The North Face, LaSportiva, and Petzl. On his personal website, he outlines how he did "Echale"—an 8b+—when he was 14, leading on to bouldering many 8b's to 8b+'s, including two 8c's, which were first ascents. In addition, he put up "Jade" and "In Search of Time Loss," 8c's, by the age of 18. He is also a talented sport climber, having completed classic routes such as "Super Tweak," 8c, as well as "Necessary Evil," 8c+ (the first of this grade in the United States), following this up by 8c+ to 9a climbs across the globe. Also, as he puts it, though he loves the outdoors, he also enjoys the competitive nature of competitions (Woods, 2010)—hence his coming in second and third place at two bouldering World Cups, taking the silver medal at the World Cup in Vail, Colorado, in 2009, and then winning the Mammut National Championships in Salt Lake City, Utah. As climbing journalist Fox (2011a) reports, in 2010, Woods won that year's Vail Cup; however, he did not make the 2011 finals, finishing the semifinals in 11th place (Fox, 2011a). Recently, he has been putting up V13 and V14 boulder problems in Colorado. Woods has also, for the first time in the United States, given a suggested V16 to a short granite roof, "The Game," in Boulder Canyon, Colorado, which is an amazing achievement. A number of young boulderers are currently making climbing news. Recently, Carlo Traversi made the second ascent of Woods's "The Game":

On Saturday, amongst a group of elite Boulder climbers, including Dave Graham, Traversi linked the moves and finished the problem, after about five days of work. "I can't even put an estimate on the number of attempts it took," Traversi says. "I figured out the top section pretty quickly, and the key to the boulder came down to the first two foot moves. It required a unique balance of power and body positioning." (Fox, 2011g, para. 1)

As well as climbing, Woods also enjoys skating, playing basketball, traveling, running, and jumping off high ledges (Woods, 2011).

adam ondra (1993–)

"On March 27th, in the Spanish hotspot of Oliana, Czech wonderboy Adam Ondra did the first ascent of *Chaxi Raxi* (5.15b) and roughly one hour later onsighted *Blanquita*—in his own words the hardest of the five 5.14c onsights he had collected within three weeks, plus another first ascent of a 5.15a" (Kern, 2011, 57). This remarkable effort caused the young climber (active from age 6) to say that probably no one has climbed so many routes at this grade in this amount of time. He puts his climbing success partly down to having supportive parents, while others put it down to his phenomenal strength; he trains nearly all the time on bouldering walls. He is also planning to team up with Sharma to attempt "Chilam Balam," reportedly 5.15c, but given the grade of 5.15b after Ondra redpointed the route in April 2011. Previously to this, in 2010, he had done Sharma's "Golpe de Estado" (5.15b), two other 5.15a's, ten 5.14d's, nine 5.14 c's, and five 5.14b on-sights when he was just 17, as well as bouldering two V15s and five V14s (*Urban Climber*, 2011c). He also came first in the IFCS Youth World Championships in 2007 and 2008, won the FSC Lead Climbing World Cup in 2009, and the IFSC Bouldering World Cup in 2010. He was the first athlete to win both. Recent ascents include routes at Malham, UK, ranging from 8a to 9a+. Such achievements currently place him at the top of bouldering and sport climbing in the United States and globally.

On a U.S. climbing website, Ondra said about the sport, "Climbing is based on moving up. And this moving up is connected with very special feel of liberty I have never found anywhere else" (Ondra, 2011, para. 4).

---

rock climbing

the greatest climber?

The question arises whether it is possible to single out just one climber, mentioned here or outside of the list of illustrious rock climbers just compiled, who has influenced and inspired other climbers the most. Though it is not my intention to come up with a definitive ranking of the most influential person, it is interesting to look at how that decision might be reached within the culture. Climbing journalists working for the U.S. magazine *Rock and Ice*, for example, looked over 25 years of back issues to see if one climber stood out above all others:

> The usual names popped up and hovered in the form of "maybe."
> Lynn Hill, Royal Robbins, Reinhold Messner, all people who exerted a whopping influence on the sport, but could you say they affected it more than any other? These folks usually excelled at a single discipline—rock, ice or alpine. Would a polymath like Jeff Lowe . . . by virtue of his wide range of talents, outrank the likes of Todd Skinner, who was a visionary rock climber but arguably less influential because he was specialized? (Jackson, 2009b, 12)

John Long was the name they arrived at as the most influential climber, due to his ascents in California in the 1970s and his connection with the

Reinhold Messner, pictured on a plateau of Germany's highest mountain Zugspitz in southern Germany. (AP/Wide World Photos)

Stonemasters, putting up the first free ascent, with Bachar and Ron Kauk, of the 11-pitch "Astroman," as well as the first one-day ascent of El Capitan with Bridwell and Billy Westbay. He was also chosen due to the richness of his climbing writing. As Long said himself in a history of the Stonemasters, "It was all part of proving that we mattered, that we were worth a damn as human beings" (cited in Jackson, 2009b, 12).

Conversely, however, climbers sometimes refuse to accept the tag of "greatest climber of all time." Reinhold Messner, thought by many to be the world's greatest mountaineer, argues, "It's impossible to compare climbs of the 1930s to the 1970s to today. ... Each climber is only a key figure in his own time. There is no such thing as 'single greatest climbing achievement' or 'greatest climber' of all time" (cited in Jackson, 2011b, 10). It is also important to keep in mind that for most climbers, climbing involves setting themselves small goals and enjoying the process of attempting to achieve them, if possible. Moreover, for some young climbers, a parent, a sibling, or a friend, for example, may be the person that inspired them the most. Of course, heroes do not have to be famous to be influential.

6.   technicalities

rock climbing can be a highly technical sport. The technicalities of climbing can be seen in relation to a number of areas. These include the gear and equipment needed to climb safely and effectively in the confidence that the protection one has chosen is up to the job. The historical development of gear and equipment is important to note. For example, pitons made from high-strength carbon steel were a technological breakthrough in the 1940s, but climbers today can choose from a bewildering assortment of climbing gear and a multitude of pieces of equipment. While having the appropriate equipment certainly plays an important role in enabling a climber to achieve his or her goals, purchasing the most expensive or fashionable gear does not necessarily make a good climber a great one. For this, dedication and hard work on technique and performance, nutrition, and focus and motivation are essential.

gear and equipment

Engaging in rock climbing as a leisure pursuit can breed "gear freaks," or those who are obsessive in their consumption of new products and equipment. A British female climber, Mandy Kirkpatrick, writes about her gear-freak boyfriend:

> In those post-coital special moments when a woman tends to gaze lovingly at her man and ask him what he's thinking, Jack used to have the decency to think of a suitable reply such as "how much I love you" ... But, after five years together, he doesn't bother. Now I get the reply, "I was wondering what size Friend I'd need for that problem on Stanage," or simply, "crampons." (Kirkpatrick, 1997, 78)

When does a climber cross over from being rightly concerned
with the science and technicalities of his or her gear for safety
and performance reasons to being a gear freak, often indulging
in overconsumption in the process? Kirkpatrick (1997) also tells
how staff in a climbing shop at that time were so obsessed with
whether the Buffalo layering system was the better one, as
opposed to Gore-tex and fleece, that to test this, half the staff
jumped into a lake in February dressed in Buffalo, the other half
in fleece and Gore-tex, to see which dried out the quickest!

However, while the climbing industry produces a plethora of equipment, the simple act of climbing requires minimal equipment. For many,
a pair of shoes is the most essential item. Talk to most climbers, and it is
their climbing shoes that prompt them to recall memories of past climbs
and the experiences had. A pair of shoes is often the possession that climbers become the most attached to. Shoes are the only necessary equipment
for a climber soloing a route or bouldering, as a pair of shoes with sticky
rubber soles allows purchase on the rock to be climbed. However, if one
wants to start doing routes more safely and more technically, or do longer
climbs, it is necessary to consider a whole raft of other gear and equipment. And, of course, the list of necessary and optional equipment varies
depending on the type and style of climbing.

For example, a climber interested in bouldering would most likely use a
chalk bag with chalk to reduce hand sweat and increase the hold on the
rock; some also use crash pads (or bouldering mats, as they are called in
the United Kingdom) to cushion any falls. In comparison, a sport climber
needs a harness (one that can be sat in case the climber needs to rest while
doing a climb) and a belay device (which is attached to the belayer's harness with a carabiner, a piece of metal shaped in a U). The carabiner needs
to be one that can be locked, not one that just snaps shut; this allows the
rope to go through so it can be paid out or drawn in as required by the
person climbing. In addition, quickdraws (sometimes called extenders),
which are a sling made of tough nylon, are needed to place into the metal
bolts set into the wall or rock to enable a climb (Oxlade, 2003).

A rope is a necessity for either sport or trad climbing. While ropes vary
in length, most have an inner nylon core, which is encased for protection
against rope drag. Though some climbers may choose not to wear a
helmet, either because they are sport climbing, which is safer than trad

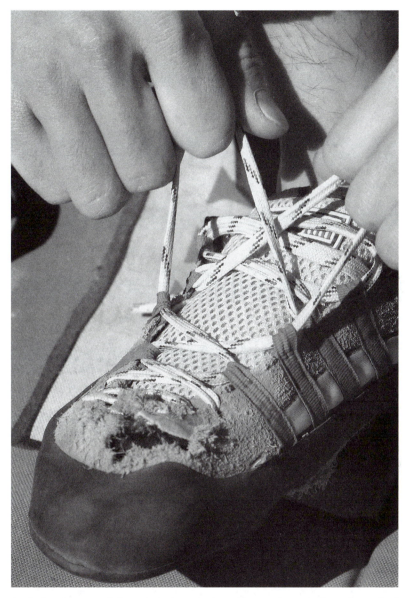

A climber laces a sticky-soled shoe designed to provide a better grip against rock surfaces. The design of such shoes has changed over the years. (AP/ Wide World Photos)

Ice climbing, shown here in Ouray, Colorado, requires extensive equipment such as an axe and crampons. (Adam Pastula)

climbing, or sometimes for reasons of fashion, a helmet protects the climber from both a fall and any loose rocks that might end up on the climber's head. Trad climbers who are leading also need to use protection to place in gaps and cracks in the rock and therefore need to place devices such as a spring-loaded cam, sometimes called a "friend," as is more common in countries such as the United Kingdom. This device is made up of three or four cams mounted on a common axle or two adjacent axles. The cams spread apart when the axle is pulled, and when a small handle is pulled the cams move together. When the device is placed into a pocket or crack in the rock, the small handle then enables the cams to expand. A climbing rope can then be attached to a sling and carabiner at the end of the stem of the device. If a climber should fall, this channels the pulling force along the stem of the unit into outward pressure on the rock. Further, the friction thus created (if the cam is properly placed) keeps the protection in place. Other protection devices include nuts, where pieces of metal of varying sizes are wedged into cracks and the rope is clipped to a wire hoop attached to the nut. "Hexes" are used in protection for larger cracks; these are six-sided metal tubes that are placed in the crack (Oxlade, 2003).

An ice climber typically needs a whole host of specialized equipment, including crampons to fix to boots to allow purchase when climbing on the ice, ice tools or axes, and ice screws as well as technical clothing such as waterproof and insulated jackets and gloves. Due to the risk of the activity, helmets are considered more of a necessity for ice climbers than in most other branches of climbing.

Additional gear needs are always determined by the style of climbing being done and the weather conditions expected. Rucksacks, haul bags, head torches, rope bags to stop ropes kinking and getting fouled up, sleeping bags, camping equipment, cameras to record an epic climb, and a hand drill for bolting your own route may also be used depending on the climb and the climber.

While it is possible to climb in jeans and a t-shirt, climbing clothing has become increasingly technical. In the wake of World War II, climbers had an excess of ex-army equipment to use, including standardized Vibram-soled army shoes at $5, tennis sneakers, and baggy army pants (Jones, 1997, 175). In addition, women often still climbed in skirts!

In contrast to the early climbers, who often had little option as to the clothing worn, contemporary climbers can choose clothing in an array of styles and colors and at a wide range of prices. Both women and men can purchase clothing designed specifically for them. However, many companies continue to employ stereotypical gendered color schemes (for example, pink and pastels for female climbers). While a large number of manufacturers now design "cool" and contemporary sportswear for different types of climbing and for different groups of climbers (for example, women, men, and children), fashion is only one element to be considered. With more technical climbs or extreme conditions, the right clothing can mean the difference between life and death. Outdoor clothing manufacturers are always updating clothing designs and using the most advanced technological materials, allegedly to maximize sporting performance and give an athletic fit.

An example of this is when the manufacturer Lowe Alpine updated Polartec's Power Stretch fabric so it was lighter when used as either a base or middle layer, depending on the weather conditions; for example, tights in this fabric are designed ergonomically for the climber's ease of movement (Rickaby, 2005). Whether such adjustments increase the grade that may be climbed is debatable. Also, climbing clothing has gone mainstream, so that someone wearing a down jacket, such as the ones manufactured by North Face, may not climb at all but likes the trendy image such climbing clothing creates. Climbers themselves have to take partial responsibility for the mainstreaming of their sport in this way. The climber Kaydee Summers comments on male climbers' apparel worn every day, even when not climbing: "Black Diamond, Arc' Teryx, and Patagonia make t-shirts for men that feature climbing icons of sorts. They are meant to just be worn around daily life, but allow guys to advertise their favourite activity" (pers. comm.).

a history of essential equipment

In this section we look particularly at three essential, and often controversial, pieces of gear: ropes, harnesses, and climbing shoes. The development and use of these items often causes heated debate in magazines, on forums, and among climbers themselves, with many discussions focusing on which products enable the quickest or hardest climb in as safe and efficient manner as possible. First, however, it is important to note that both the design and usage of current climbing gear and equipment has a long history with many important scientific and technological advances enabling new developments in performance and participation. The British academics Rose and Parsons, in their book *Invisible on Everest: Innovation and the Gear Makers* (2002), trace how climbing gear has developed over the last 150 years. Initially, Victorian mountaineers in their pursuit of first ascents in the Alps used simple but often very effective tools. Furthermore, advancements in gear made in the early 1900s can be seen as being developed in German-speaking countries.

An early example of technical climbing in the United States was Albert Ellingwood and Barton Hoag's 1920 ascent of Lizzard Head, Colorado. The ascent required the use of very primitive pitons, which have been described as "iron spikes similar to those used for steps on telegraph poles" (Jones, 1997, 103). However, at that time, Ellingwood was not able to fix the rope to the spikes, given that the carabiner had not yet been invented. Early climbers were at the forefront of some of the most important technological advances. This is evidenced by Dwight Lavender, who fashioned his own pitons in the engineering workshop at Stanford University to allow the rope to pass through due to having an open eye that was subsequently closed shut. Other key breakthroughs, such as Salathé's high-strength carbon steel pitons in the 1940s, support Mellor's (2001) view that "In the beginning, it would usually take two kinds of people to create a so-called technical rock climb: someone to declare it impossible and someone to envision a method by which to prove him wrong" (21).

In 1950, Dale Johnson, a Boulder climber, brought climbing in Colorado into the modern age by employing a two-rope system (Achey, Chelton, & Godfrey, 2002). Employing this system, Johnson managed to do "Practice Roof," the first roof climbing of its type in the region. He was also an early pioneer of the use of expansion bolts. But, as the following quote illustrates, the period of trial and error was also one of high risk for the climber and equipment pioneer: "Whispering a silent prayer and shouting 'Red alert!' to his anxious belayers, Johnson clipped in a foot sling and gingerly transferred his weight to the piton. The next instant, the piton went flying past his head and he followed it downward. As he fell he waited for the jerk of his last half-driven piton being pulled out by the impact of the fall. By some miracle it held" (Achey, Chelton, & Godfrey, 2002, 23). And so new belaying techniques and better ropes would encourage such risk taking.

Different climbing areas called for diverse new inventions in climbing equipment. For example, the unique aspects of the Yosemite region required a new style of climbing, which entailed having "to master smooth jamcracks, invent specialized equipment for less-than-perfect piton cracks, and figure out a way to haul big loads up the hot, near-vertical faces" (Roper, 1994,11). More recently, in 2010, the American climbing magazine *Rock and Ice* ran a retrospective piece about the development of new equipment and technologies in Yosemite. Climbing writer Jeff Jackson recalls,

> It was 1998 and I was standing in the Camp 4 parking lot with all my gear thrown on a tarp, sorting for a trip up El Cap when a skinny old guy with dazzling white hair and a goofy smile approached and asked if I wanted to look at his nuts. He winked at the double entendre and said in a voice with the slightest Jimmy Stewart warble, "Actually they're called Sentinel Nuts. I make them with a straight taper to balance security and removability. Hi, I'm Tom Frost." He stuck his hand out and I shook it with reverence. Tom Frost! This was the guy on the cover of Royal Robbin's *Basic Rockcraft*, my bible when I was learning to climb. (Jackson, 2010c, 37)

Frost had climbed with Robbins, Chuck Pratt, and Yvon Chouinard and achieved first ascents of "Salathé Wall" and "North America Wall" during the 1960s. Further, along with Chouinard in the early 1970s, he established Great Pacific Iron Works, which is now known as Black Diamond Equipment and Patagonia Inc. As Jackson notes, Chouinard is responsible for creating much of the gear (and the techniques) that characterize modern-day climbing. (See also Chapter 5, "Heroes.")

These pioneering attempts show how individual climbers, usually with limited scientific knowledge or design skills, helped push gear developments, raising climbing standards in the process. A "gear trajectory" has been traced from the 1970s, when the Californian Ray Jardine invented a spring-loaded camming device that was inserted into cracks, which then held a climber if he or she fell if the rope was clipped through it (Wells, 2001). During this same period, there were also much improved wired metal chocks with tapered faces being made in an array of different sizes to aid with protection. Thus, even thin or flared cracks could be utilized to protect leaders, who were more open to taking a fall with the promise of better protection afforded by such devices.

With such a diversity of products currently on the market, most leading rock-climbing publications do an annual assessment of the best gear categories with their opinions sometimes supported by a panel of rock-climbing readers. Often reviews are conducted by experienced climbers comparing an array of different products. For instance, in 2009, *Rock and Ice* gave awards based on quality, safety, efficiency, and value for sunglasses that protect eyes from lichen, ice, and "ricocheting rock shards"; climbing shoes that are applauded for being "high performance" and having the necessary Vibram sole grip, which is "super sticky"; and a removable bolt to be used after a hole has been drilled in the rock, which is claimed to have "revolutionized sport climbing by making the back-breaking work of equipping bolted climbs much easier—just ask Chris Sharma, Randy Leavitt or Danni Andrada" (Jackson, 2009d, 14). A locking carabiner is also praised: "Ever notice when you belay or rappel that your locking carabiner inevitably flips sideways and for a brief instant the rope or your device rides on the locked gate? Ever wonder what would happen if at that instant the carabiner were suddenly loaded? I'll tell you what probably happens: Ping! 'Yaaaaaa!' Splat" (Raleigh, 2009b, 16). For many readers, these annual assessments inform their consumption choices leading into a climbing season.

Further, though technological innovations have altered climbing performance and safety, such developments ensure that other elements of the climbing experience have also evolved. This can be seen, for instance, in relation to debates between climbers over the ethical merits of bolting routes. This is particularly because equipment such as bolt guns, used to drill into the rock so fixed bolts can be placed, became more common and inexpensive. Such innovations are welcomed (though sometimes with ambivalence from climbers), as more often than not they have been developed by members of the climbing community themselves; many climbing equipment firms are owned and run by climbers.

gear development: harnesses, ropes, and climbing shoes

The safety and reliability of equipment is vital so climbers can make moves, sometimes beyond their present capabilities and certainly beyond their comfort zones, with some sense of confidence. Ropes and harnesses are so integral to the act of climbing that these two items are often under the gear review spotlight for their technical properties. For instance, a harness needs to be light, as any extra weight can impede a climber's progress, especially at elite levels. It must also be comfortable and very durable, as well as give good lumbar support. A survey in 2007 found that only 10 percent of climbers inspect their harnesses every time before they put them on (for wear and tear, for instance fraying) and, what's more, climbers were not aware of how old their harnesses were (Jackson, 2009a). The same piece of gear, therefore, can perform different functions, so with a harness, "Whether you're falling off, working out beta, or pulling marathon belay sessions for someone doing the same, your harness is holding your ass a lot . . . and accommodates your particular climbing style" (*Urban Climber*, 2011a, 32). In an attempt to make harnesses as light as possible, new technological and material developments are employed: "extra padding is stripped away, replaced with lightweight foam or mesh, and buckles and straps are slimmed down, leaving these rigs at 12 ounces or less . . . compared with about 16 ounces for the average all-around harness" (Fox, 2011c, 37).

Ropes are equally important to the act of climbing. While not all climbers use ropes (for example, if soloing), those using a harness will also be using at least one rope. Ropes are judged by diameter; length; weight; maximum impact force; static and dynamic elongation; how many falls a rope has held through in rigorous testing; whether a rope is single, double, or twin; and if it has been dry coated (Osius, 2009b). The development of nylon ropes after World War II was a key safety development in climbing.

Ropes can come in different lengths from a standard 50 meters, so a lower-off is possible at the 25-meter point, to 60- and 70-meter ropes.

But, in a recent review of ropes, it was pointed out that while ropes may "all look similar," the "difference in their diameters is measured in the smallest increment on a ruler, and they come in essentially two lengths: long and slightly longer. So how come there are so many opinions about which are best?" (*Urban Climber*, 2011b, 38). The same reviewer argues that ropes are very different in terms of how they coil, clip, handle, and feel, but "Since that cord connects you to your belayer and keeps you off the deck, having a strong opinion about rope preferences might not be such a bad thing" (2011b, 38). As the materials used to make ropes have become stronger and more durable, ropes have become thinner. Whereas 10 years ago lead ropes were 11 mm in diameter, they are now 10 mm as standard, with 9 mm single ropes becoming increasingly common (Osius, 2009b).

Given the diversity of products available, it is perhaps not surprising that there is no consensus about which ropes are best due to the differences in climbing styles, techniques, and individual preferences, as well as the income a climber may have. Whereas some climbers "won't even look at a 10 mm rope, others still were nervous about anything under 9.8 mm," and while "sport climbers in Colorado thought that dry treatments to ropes (if to be used on wet rock or snow) were an 'unjustifiable expense,' " ice climbers, however, "felt differently still" (Ellison, 2011, 61). A query from a reader to a climbing magazine in 2011 enquired as to "which is more important, the number of UIAA/CE falls a rope can hold, or how many kiloNewtons it can hold?" (Gear Guy, 2011, 76). The reply was a complex answer concerning how important the maximum impact force is, which is the number of kilonewtons a rope transmits onto the top piece of protection in a fall. In reality, the more a rope stretches, the lower its impact force, which is good, but as the answer points out, is not quite so good if it stretches so much the climber hits the rock! Therefore, it is also important to consider dynamic elongation, which tells you how much a rope stretches in percentage terms. This means the best rope is one that has both low dynamic elongation and a low maximum impact force (Gear Guy, 2011, 76).

Climbing shoes are arguably the most iconic piece of climbing gear. They too are evolving as the sport continues to change and diversify at a rapid pace and new standards of rock-climbing performance continue to be set. Rubber technologies have been particularly important in the development of climbing shoes. In the 1980s, the Spanish manufacturer Boreal brought out a rock shoe that had a new sticky sole with a rubber compound and so, for example, aided friction moves on rock, which pushed climbing standards higher than ever before (Wells, 2001).

Today, climbers have the choice of over 150 varieties of climbing shoes. Traditionally, climbers tended to buy either trad shoes, which were often more comfortable than sport shoes, or shoes specifically designed for sport climbing. Now, the more important criteria for choosing a pair of rock shoes is fit. For example, the famous climber Alex Honnold wears the same pair of sport shoes because of the fit so that he was able to climb 5.13 cracks and Yosemite big-wall climbs as well as shorter, steep sport routes (Weidner, 2011). Of course, not all climbers have Honnold's skill and ability to adapt to such divergent conditions. While many other climbers would change their shoes for such different conditions, the right fit is still paramount for all.

Different styles of climbing typically require different shoes. If you are sport climbing on overhanging rock, this requires a soft shoe; climbing on vertical rock typically calls for a stiffer sole; shoes need to be able to come on and off quickly when climbing indoors; getting into cracks requires a supple boot with a narrow toe; long routes call for a more comfortable shoe; and bouldering needs a shoe that is secure but also goes on easily (Bisharat, 2009a). Perhaps the most common gear-related debate among climbers is about how tight or snug a shoe should be for optimum performance. For instance, are they tight enough so the foot does not move around but loose enough not to cause much pain? Performance can be hindered by such issues. Climbers, however, have been known to suffer intense pain if they feel it will help them climb a route the next grade up from their current one. However, modern technological advances have meant that "The days when you had to buy your shoes two sizes too small and stretch them to fit are long gone" (Goodlad, 2005, 68). The ultimate rock shoe is that which combines comfort and precision.

As well as fit to the foot and conditions, a rock shoe's grip is paramount so a climber can use his or her shoes to gain the best purchase on the rock, for example when using the technique of "smearing." On slab climbing, for instance, this entails getting as much contact on the rock with the sole of the shoe as is possible, to create friction. If soles start to lose their grip but the rock shoes themselves are in good shape, then the process of oxidation has occurred through the act of climbing, causing the rubber to harden, get slicker, and grind off (Gear Guy, 2010). From an environmental and recycling point of view, rather than buying new ones, shoes can be resoled for around a third of the cost of a new pair, or soles can be self-sanded.

gear, danger, risk, and ethics

Climbing gear and equipment can also raise both safety and ethical issues. For instance, pure climbing chalk (first used by climbers in California in the 1970s) is magnesium carbonate ($MgCO_3$), originally sold for constipation and indigestion. It is not a known carcinogen, though it can be, according to the U.S. Department of Labor, a respiratory hazard: "Think of it as a poor man's Ex-lax. Eating chalk isn't going to harm you, but it can literally have you crapping yourself over that big unclimbed block you found deep in the woods" (Gear Guy, 2009, 72). Others think that the excessive use of chalk can be unsightly in environmental terms, spoiling the natural appearance of the rock if used too liberally.

Climbing is a risk sport (see Chapter 1, "Explanations"). And though the intention may be to minimize risk (in contrast to media-fuelled images of risk-taking stunt devils), safety is an issue in relation to gear for both indoor climbing in the gym and climbing outdoors. For example, in 2010, two climbers were on "Yellow Spur" (5.10a) on Redgarden Wall in Eldorado Canyon, Colorado, when a belayer, who was anchored to a tree, paid out slack on the rope. After putting in a cam at some difficult 5.8 moves, the lead climber fell. The gear did not hold; the rope pulled tight, as if the fall was being slowed, but the rope stretched and then severed. The lead climber fell 80 feet to his death (Jackson, 2011c). So, though accidents can be attributed to human error (for example, an inexperienced or inattentive belayer not tying in correctly by using a well-knotted bowline or trace-eight knot, or due to a leader placing gear badly), they can also be due, as was the case here, to gear not performing as expected.

Indoor climbing can also be a dangerous activity. Sometimes climbers wear weight belts to make training harder by carrying extra pounds as they climb. Mark Hipshire, a climber from Knoxville, Tennessee, recalled how another climber's weight belt slipped off, fell about 40 feet, and hit him on the head. This resulted in a concussion, a 3.5-inch cut, three chipped teeth, and the need to have treatment from a chiropractor to alleviate crunched vertebrae due to whiplash sustained as a result of the accident (Hipshire, 2010, 10–11). Climbing magazines often have an accident report section. It allows readers to learn from the mistakes of other climbers and promotes a safety-conscious ethos throughout the climbing community. Climbers committed to safety can also take first-aid or general medical courses, which are tailored for climbers in different capacities, for example, as an instructor or just as an individual who is safety conscious.

Moreover, in a consumerist, media-image-driven society, ethically, how much is too much gear? What are the messages given out through advertising and television regarding how sport is both sold as a commodity and used to sell consumer goods to the mass public (see, for example, Cashmore, 2000)? Jackson notes, "This January, I wandered around the gargantuan mall that is the Outdoor Retailer trade show in Salt Lake, a paean to consumerism, where the gods of selling and spending are lavishly feted by adoring PR people, retail buyers and media . . . 'All this crap, I thought. I don't need any of it' " (Jackson, 2009c, 10). And yet, when he reflected back on an earlier climbing life, when he was a climber with a hippie goatee and ponytail, dressed in tie-dye clothing, he calculated that he owned $150 rock shoes, mountain shoes, haul bags, two harnesses, cams, headlamps, ropes, numerous belay and rappel devices, two sleeping bags, jackets, crampons, balaclavas, bib overalls, ice tools, a drill with anchor materials, bolts for new routes, ascenders, tents, and packs. In his own words, "I liked to think that I existed outside the world of money, consumerism and the tinselled American glut of the 1990s, but in fact, gear—and the climbing it enabled—gave my life meaning" (10). Continuing, Jackson makes the plea, even in the current climate of a financial downturn, not to take away his climbing gear: "That's all I really

---

Within the climbing culture, there are interesting ethical debates about who gets to keep lost or left-behind gear at a crag. A chart in *Urban Climber* magazine (2010) entitled "The Booty Matrix" raises these issues (with a sense of irony), stating that it might be considered ethical to take home a single carabiner or quick link found partially up a bolted sport route due to the fact that it was most likely left by climbers who got in over their heads and then bailed out. However, if it was found on the anchors, then it was probably left for other climbers to use and so should not be taken, though it could be generously replaced if it looks old or worn out. On the other hand, more straightforwardly, if a crash pad (which is used to cushion a fall) is stashed or hidden away, climbing ethics, if followed, would deem that this specific piece of gear is not "booty," though even here there is room for ethical doubt. What, for instance, if the crash pad is causing an environmental or access risk? The advice is to return it with a warning if possible, but, if it happens again, it's yours!

need . . . gear and salsa" (10). This example also raises the question of how extreme sports in general and rock climbing in particular can exclude certain groups because of the costs of participating—for example, those on low incomes. Climbing can be an expensive pursuit for purchasing even a basic kit of shoes, rope, and harness, for example. Of course, this doesn't include travel costs to and from a site.

training and nutrition for climbing performance

So you think the Body Beautiful's some new product like Pepsi Max, huh? Get real! Remember Lytton Strachey's lucubration's over the divine statuesque body, of George Leigh Mallory? Ok, so we're talking decorative there—aesthetic appreciation and all that. But the idea of training for the sport's been around for longer than you might think, and conjecture about the ideal body type for particular aspects of mountain activity for even longer. (*Climber*, 1997, 32)

Many contemporary elite and non-elite climbers recognize training as integral to performance. However, it was not until the 1960s that climbers really began to adopt a systematic approach to training. For example, in Britain, the climber Pete Livesey transferred the training techniques of athletics to rock climbing. In the United States, John Gill, renowned as the founder of American bouldering, was also known for applying gymnastic techniques and chalk to rock climbing (Ament, 1992).

> **Climbing techniques range from "crimping," which is climbing using only the fingers, to "bridging," which is climbing a corner having the legs spread apart, to "dynoing," which is making a dynamic or explosive and dramatic move to a hold beyond your reach.**

Contemporary training covers a multitude of activities, including diet and nutrition. As Franklin (2009) observes, there is no doubt that climbing is a physically demanding sport where muscles are continually breaking down and rebuilding. With this in mind, considering the types and kinds of protein in the diet, such as beef, soy, and poultry, is important, as is knowing which are the best carbohydrates that convert to glucose or blood sugar to give energy, such as whole grains rather than simple sugars (for example, white bread), which end up burning more quickly. The quality of fats is also important nutritionally, and here Franklin suggests that no more than 30 percent of a climber's daily calorie intake should consist of unsaturated fats (for example, salmon or olive oil) and to avoid "bad" saturated fats (for example, bacon). A healthy climber's diet should also include a variety of vegetables for vitamins and antioxidants. As with many other sports, there is considerable debate among committed and professional climbers as to whether they should support their sporting diets with vitamin supplements.

As well as meeting the nutritional needs of the climbing body, an awareness of psychology can also aid and enhance climbers' training and overall performance. Some climbers are even employing psychological skills training (for example, imagery, goal setting, and arousal-regulation strategies) to gain the competitive edge. One aspect that has received attention from sports psychologists has been the use of imagery in rock climbing. Imagery refers to how a climber uses all his or her senses to recreate or create an experience in the mind. This is a valuable skills technique that can enhance sporting performance in terms of energy and technique. It might involve, for instance, imagining working through a climbing problem while having an injury, so that the climber is in control of a potentially negative situation (Boyd & Munroe, 2003). Further study has been carried out on the psychological techniques employed by elite mountaineers to be able to advance their climbing goals. The mountaineers' levels of focus, capacity for mental imagery, short-term goal-setting skills, and self-belief levels all contributed to their strategies for climbing success (Burke & Orlick, 2003).

Training also includes stretching exercises to improve flexibility, power and power endurance exercises, and strength exercises to improve such aspects as core strength (which is important to climb well) through activities such as Pilates. Many climbers also train regularly in climbing gyms to push forward technique, endurance, and stamina. But, according to Doyle (2009), many climbers do so without sufficient knowledge, such as the difference between strength and power. He defines strength as the maximum contraction that a muscle can exert, and power as the strength of muscle groups to complete a movement when climbing in as short a time as is needed. Activities such as system boards, campusing, and bouldering build up a climber's strength. A system board is a board with differently sized and spaced holds on it and is a good method of repeating the same movement on the same holds, which allows you to measure your climbing progress, as all the variables are fixed. Campusing is power training done on a campus board, using only the arms. Such exercises, Doyle outlines, allow climbers to use the muscle power they have in the most productive way, but the effect these give eventually plateaus, and then, he says, more strength is needed if a climber wants to see further improvements.

The level of prowess and commitment of a climber dictates what kinds of exercise will best improve an individual's performance. For example, it determines whether power or strength exercises should be focused on at any one time, as well as the frequency and repetition of such exercises over a specific time frame, for instance of weeks or of months, with long-term training meant to "coordinate physical, mental and skill cycles to produce a period of peak performance" (Wright, 2009, 68). For less elite climbers, the aim may well be to keep up a more consistent and longer rise in performance. But there are risks to training, as Neil Gresham (2009) argues, as overtraining can lead to performance plateauing out, and then injuries can occur. Determining the best training routine for any individual climber is not, however, an exact science, and argument rages as to what are the best training methods for optimum climbing performance and for specific goals. Also, training, at times, can encourage climbers to become obsessively scientific in terms of what, when, and in what sequence the best exercises are to be performed.

A British view of how American climbers train, at least in the late 1990s, was summed up by a (partly) tongue-in-cheek, stereotypical account in a British climbing magazine at the time. In the account, Americans were summed up as self-obsessed, humorless, and keen to be the best at any cost, including taking large amounts of chemical substances (*Climber*, 1997, 34).

What was not a joke was the effects of overtraining for some climbers at that time, with an increase in male bulimia and anorexia. More recently, in the United States, this has led to weigh-ins at climbing competitions, when, in 2008, Austria's climbing federation was emphatic that any competitors who had a body-mass index (BMI) of less than 17 were banned from competing. Robin Erbesfield, the winner of four World Cup titles, admitted that due to strength-to-weight ratio being fundamental to climbers' success, eating disorders are a way of life for some top-class climbing athletes. Some climbing journalists have asked whether the IFSC, or indeed any climbing organization, has any responsibility to intervene in this issue (Snider, 2009). There are also arguments as to whether BMI is the best way to look for evidence of eating disorders, as it is not a foolproof method. However, whatever the debates, climbing coach

David Verderrosa (cited in Snider, 2009) argues that if a climber is too skinny over a long period of time, his or her climbing suffers due to chronic fatigue, not to mention hair loss and brittle nails.

As discussed in Chapter 3, "Science," avoiding injury is of paramount importance for a climber at whatever level, and particularly for elite or professional climbers in their training program. Thus, avoiding "belayer's neck," a dislocated shoulder, finger tears, and impact trauma on ankles, for instance, are important considerations if a climber does not want to spend the season resting while friends push up their grades and enjoy themselves. (See Chapter 1, "Explanations" for the international grading system that climbers use to judge their sporting progress.) Good training techniques, or reassessment of old ones, is key to avoiding such injuries in the first place and to effective climbing performance.

In referring to the overall findings of the first International Conference on Science and Technology in Climbing and Mountaineering, held in the United Kingdom in 1999, Smith (2000) selected a number of conclusions from the conference. A key finding was that not many injured climbers go to their doctors for help. Also, many climbers who do actually seek medical assistance then find it hard to responsibly apply the suggested treatment methods of rehabilitation and rest.

Therefore, the best training methods based on scientific *and* anecdotal evidence will eventually become ineffective for climbing performance if a climber chooses to either ignore or not seek sound medical advice, or forgets that rest and rehabilitation when needed is just what the (climbing) doctor ordered!

Climbing training may still lag behind other, more fully professional sports, such as athletics, tennis, or basketball. However, in recent years, there has been a quantum leap in recognizing the importance of training, correct technique, diet, psychological strategies, and injury prevention and treatment on the performance and enjoyment of both elite and non-elite climbers involved in the sport. Climbers themselves, though, have a canny way of distilling all this advice from a variety of sources down into a workable and commonsense mantra, as this climber posting on a forum demonstrates: "The lessons seem obvious: 1. Make quick decisions based on experience and the information in front of you. 2. Be adaptable in your approach and take what the route gives you. 3. Clip when you can and don't waste energy doing it. 4. Make continuous upward progress" (Lipinski, 2011, para. 10). Though he also says that doing this is another thing entirely!

7.   futures

since the first mountains and rock faces were scaled in the United States in the nineteenth century, the sport has seen many changes. These have included more people in general entering the sport, especially women and young adults, some of them achieving at high levels. In addition, the commercialization of extreme sports and climbing in particular has relatively recently occurred. This is evidenced in the sponsorship of elite climbers by gear manufacturers or outdoor clothing companies.

Increasingly, extreme sports and climbing in particular form a growing industry. Climbing is now a highly profitable business, and this can be seen in individuals who make their living from the sport as roped access workers, climbing gym employees, climbing instructors and guides, and professional climbers, for instance. Also, the aforementioned climbing equipment and clothing companies, climbing media and publishers, climbing literature and film festivals, climbing holiday packages, membership in climbing gyms, and climbing competitions are all part of the spin-off activities that increasingly surround the sport.

Rock climbing has emerged since the pioneering exploits of those early mountaineers into a full-blown lifestyle sport. The consideration of sport climbing and bouldering for inclusion in the 2020 Olympic Games is further proof that the sport has entered the mainstream. The globalization of climbing has seen climbers now travelling outside their own countries to far-flung destinations such as Thailand, China, Patagonia, Vietnam, Peru, Australia, and New Zealand, to name but a few. The ethical implications of climbing in countries where, for example, low wages and poverty exist is something that Western climbers will increasingly have to grapple with as the visiting of these destinations increases.

There have been significant historical shifts as well, from aid to free climbing, and the development specifically of sport climbing, bouldering, and indoor and outdoor climbing competitions. In such competitions, participants compete with each other, sometimes for material gain. Developments in gear and equipment, as well as specialist climbing clothing due to more advanced technology and innovative design, have helped push climbing standards further than ever before. The advances made in training, nutrition, and techniques have ensured that the top climbers in the United States and elsewhere are recognized as high-performing athletes. It will be interesting to see just how much elite climbers can outdo the current established climbing grades in different areas of the sport because of these developments. Furthermore, technological changes in how the sport is accessed through personal and commercial climbing blogs and websites, and the digitalization of the climbing media, all serve to make information about the sport easier to access and increase participation.

Environmental issues have always been at the heart of American climbing. This can be witnessed in the early efforts of the conservationist John Muir in the nineteenth century, when he campaigned for the preservation of wilderness and wild lands.

Many years later, the climber Amy Irvine (2002) pleads, "What an indomitable force we could be, if we collectively bellowed a deafening, fearless No! to the vanishing of wilderness and other critical habitats" (203).Thus, individual and collective efforts to preserve the wilderness, and therefore the climbing environment, for future generations have occurred both in the past and in more recent times.

This intention to maintain the uniqueness of the American rock-climbing scene could also be seen when Chris McNamara started the American Safe Climbing Association in 1998. This was designed to clean up and minimize the environmental and visual effects of unsafe climbing anchors (bolts) left behind on walls. Climbers themselves run the organization on a nonprofit basis (see http://www.safeclimbing.org/). Today, a number of organizations are concerned to continue to protect the climbing environment for those rock climbers not even yet born.

Another unresolved environmental issue that has ethical implications for the future of climbing is the use of chalk. Used to make fingers drier, it has the unintended consequence of making the rock look unsightly. It can also give an indication of how the route should be done. This could be seen as aiding the climber but also as taking away the route-finding element of a climb (Wells, 2001). The future of the environment is also at stake in the question of what happens to old climbing gear when it is no longer needed. The recycling advice given for an old rope varies from

Yosemite National Park ranger Jesse McGahey inspects an abandoned rope at the base of El Capitan in 2007. Evidence of rock climbing's excesses are visible everywhere around the base of popular summer ascents here. Dead pines lie decomposing on the eroded rock, their roots exposed by thousands of boot soles. In a single month, volunteers packed out 900 pounds of abandoned rope, snack wrappers, and toilet paper strewn around some of Yosemite's most cherished crags. But as climbers head to national parks to test their skills in the great outdoors, some are breaking the wilderness ethic that has long governed the sport. (AP/Wide World Photos)

the suggestions to use a rope bag to make it last longer by protecting it, to retire the rope if it is very frayed or has been exposed to chemicals, to up-cycle it by making a rope rug, or to recycle it via one of the rope companies (Snider, 2011).

The question of access to land and rock for climbers has been an issue since climbing began and continues to be so. Therefore, a future concern is to ensure that climbers have such access to allow them to climb responsibly.

One area that has had access issues in the past is the climbing area of the "Gunks." The Shawangunk Ridge is a very intricate mix of private and public lands. Each area here has different rules and regulations for would-be climbers to understand if they intend climbing there. However, local activists have plans to ensure that climbing is revitalized through the development of a brand new area:

> This Saturday, May 22, the Gunks Climbers Coalition, in concert with the Mohonk Preserve and the Access Fund, is hosting a party to raise money to purchase Waterworks, a newly discovered 175-acre area with world-class bouldering and route climbing on still largely undeveloped cliffs, located in Rosendale, just north of the Gunks. (Bisharat, 2010b, para. 3)

Local and regional activism such as this demonstrates that the institutionalism, regulation, and commercialization of the sport can be, and is being, resisted. In contrast to this, Mellor's (2001) view is that despite the rich diversity of American climbing, there still exists "the insidious homogenization that is erasing the regional distinctiveness in every facet of American culture, rock climbing included" (9). However, the Gunks' example above demonstrates that the spirit of the maverick, antiestablishment, antimainstream climber is alive and well.

Climbing activism can also be seen more globally, as the example of the Austrian climber Gerhard Schaar in India demonstrates. In 2005, he visited the granite domes and spires of the climbing area of Ramanagaram, situated 60 miles west of Mysore. Though it was an area with great climbing potential, he was concerned for his local Indian friends' safety when they were attempting to put up new routes. Therefore, in 2008, he returned with a drill and gear to teach them how to equip routes both safely and properly (Jackson, 2010a). Thus, the future of the sport in respect of the aforementioned local and global trends is contradictory in its effects, and the outcomes are far from certain.

It is more certain that generally, and specifically in a U.S. context, extreme sports are still mostly white, wealthy, and exclusionary. Participation in extreme sports still demands that individuals have leisure time, funds, and access to specialized sporting environments (Rinehart & Sydnor, 2003). Such sports are also still predominantly heterosexual in constitution. How currently excluded groups, such as people of color or the poor, are to be given both access and encouragement to participate in a sport such as rock climbing is an important consideration for the future.

The question of future developments in climbing can be seen, therefore, in relation to environmental issues, access, and the need to widen out the sport's demographics. However, the question can also be interpreted as how an individual climber might anticipate the future and any personal "climbing journey" in the sport.

Climbing writer Bisharat (2010a) reflects on a "number of watershed experiences" that the climber can expect to encounter "upon tying in for the long haul." These experiences include the first time someone defines themselves as a "real climber," the first time they climb El Cap, the first time they have a "lead fall," the first time a friend is lost through climbing, and the first time they get injured. All these facets of the climbing experience may await the aspiring or new climber. Finally, the ultimate future destination of any individual's climbing journey is seen as when there is no longer any need to call oneself a climber because you "just are one": "You do it, because it's what you do. Climbing is just you, going up" (Bisharat, 2010a, para. 14).

glossary

aac. American Alpine Club.

adventure climbing. *See* Traditional (trad) climbing.

aid climbing. The use of equipment on a route—for example, nuts and slings to allow for the climber to progress on the climb.

belay. A place, often on the top of a cliff or a ledge, where a climber attaches himself/herself to the rock to allow him/herself to belay another climber.

belayer or belaying. Taking in or paying out the rope to allow another to climb while protecting him or her from falling.

beta. Information given by climbers regarding a route.

bolt. A piece of steel that is fixed into the rock and allows the rope to go through.

bouldering. Climbing without ropes on large boulders.

bmc. British Mountaineering Council.

bridge. To stretch the legs across two different points on the rock.

cam. Generic name for a protection device made of metal placed into cracks.

carabiner. A shaped ring made of metal that allows other pieces of gear to be clipped to it. Sometimes called a biner.

chalk. Magnesium chalk usually placed in a chalk bag to aid a climber's grip.

climbing gym/wall. An indoor constructed climbing venue.

crack.   A small fissure in the rock.

crack climbing.   Climbing where hands and feet are wedged into the rock.

crag.   An area where climbing occurs.

crimping.   A very small finger hold.

crux.   The hardest section on a climb.

deep-water soloing.   Climbing on sea cliffs and using the sea to land.

dyno.   A dynamic leap for a climbing hold.

face climbing.   Climbing over the face of a rock.

flash.   To climb a route on the first attempt without falling or practicing first.

free climbing.   Climbing without direct use of equipment.

friend.   A protection device.

gear.   Climbing equipment.

harness.   A device made of nylon that supports the climber when on a route and that is attached to the rope.

headpointing.   Leading a traditional climb after practicing on a top rope.

ice climbing.   Climbing on ice using equipment such as crampons and ice axes.

ifsc.   International Federation of Sport Climbing.

imcf.   International Mountaineering and Climbing Federation.

jamming.   Climbing by jamming in various parts of the body, for example, a fist.

lead climbing/leader.   The climber who goes up a route first, clipping into the rope for protection.

nut.   A protection device used in traditional climbing.

offwidth.   A crack that does not allow for secure jamming.

on-sight.   To lead a climb with no prior knowledge.

overhang.   Steep rock that sticks outwards.

pinkpoint.   To lead a route without falling but where protection is placed beforehand.

piton.   A spike made of metal hammered into rock.

protection.   Gear placed on the rock to prevent or minimize falls.

pumped.   When a climber's arms are tired from being on a climb.

quickdraw.   A piece of gear consisting of a nylon sling with a carabiner at each end.

rack.   The climber's gear collection.

rappel.   Descending from a route by using a braking device to slide down the rope.

redpoint.   A term used especially in sport climbing where a route is done after practice, for example after toproping initially.

rock shoes/boots.   Shoes designed for climbing with a sticky rubber sole to aid friction on the rock.

second.   The climber who ascends a route second.

slab climbing.   Very smooth and less-than-vertical rock necessitating effective footwork.

soloing.   Climbing with no equipment apart from rock boots and perhaps chalk.

sport climbing.   Climbing on rock that is equipped and protected with a line of preplaced bolts.

toprope.   When climbing is done by a rope that is attached to a belay above or is paid out by the climber who leads the route.

traditional (trad) climbing.   Climbing on rock where there are no bolts already in place and the lead climber places protection.

bibliography

Achey, J., Chelton, D., & Godfrey, B. (2002). *Climb! The History of Rock Climbing in Colorado*. Seattle, WA: The Mountaineers Books.

Ament, P. (1992). *Master of Rock: A Lighthearted Walk through the Life and Rock Climbing of John Gill*. Lincoln, NE: Adventures Meaning Press.

Ament, P. (1999, December). "Heroes: Royal Robbins." *Rock and Ice* 97, 68–79.

Ament, P. (2002a). "Reflections on Being the Best Climber in the World," in P. Ament (ed.), *Climber's Choice* (pp. 120–45). New York: Ragged Mountain Press.

Ament, P. (2002b). *A History of Free Climbing in America: Wizards of Rock*. Berkeley, CA: Wilderness Press.

Ament, P. (2002c). "Foreword to John Sherman," in P. Ament (ed.), *Climber's Choice* (p. 8). New York: Ragged Mountain Press.

American Safe Climbing Association. (2003). "Rock Climbing and Rock Protection/Anchors." Retrieved February 22, 2012 from http://www.safeclimbing.org/about_overview.htm.

Anna, T., Jan, B., and Aleksander, T. (2007). "Goals in Sports Career and Motivation as the Measure of Professionalism in Snowboarding." *Medicina Sportiva* 11, 27–31.

Arce, G. (1996). *Defying Gravity: High Adventure on Yosemite's Walls*. Berkeley, CA: Wilderness Press.

Averbeck, C. (2011, May). "Deep Wisdom: A New Way of Thinking in the Old South." *Climbing*, 38–45.

Bahrke, S. M., and Shukitt-Hale, B. (1993). "Effects of Altitude on Mood, Behaviour and Cognitive Functioning." *Sports Medicine* 16, 97–125.

Baker, M. (2010, July). "Vintage Vantage." *Rock and Ice* 187, 56–63.

Baláš, J. (2005). "Influence of Climbing Activities on Child Physical Fitness," in Jiří Baláš, Ondřej Pohanka, and Ladislav Vomáčko (eds.), *Proceedings from 2nd International Mountain and Outdoor Sports Conference* (pp. 79–85). Hruba Skala, Czech Republic.

Barkam, P. (2010, December 15). "Dude, You Gotta Cut Your Arm Off." *The Guardian* (6–10).

Barlow, A. (2009, December). "Climb to Live, Live to Climb." *Rock and Ice* 182, 17.

Bayers, P. L. (2003). *Imperial Ascent: Mountaineering, Masculinity and Empire*. Boulder, CO: University Press of Colorado.

Bisharat, A. (2009a). "Foot Sense: Getting the Most Out of the One Thing that Can Make You Climb Better." *Rock and Ice* 177, 42–49.

Bisharat, A. (2009b, April). "Regime Change." *Rock and Ice* 176, 16.

Bisharat, A. (2010a). "Milestones." *Evening Sends* (blog). Retrieved August 10, 2011, from http://eveningsends.com/2011/05/milestones/.

Bisharat, A. (2010b). "Upcoming Event/Party." *BASECAMP: . . . Where Every Climber Starts*, 24. Retrieved November 4, 2010, from http://mail.blueyonder.co.uk/mail/?AuthEventSource=SSO#search/shawangunks/128b7b2e6e2e0429.

Bisharat, A. (2010c, October). "What I've Learned: Beth Rodden" *Rock and Ice* 189, 36.

Bisharat, A. (2010d, July 26). "Guys' Weekend and the Third Day On." Retrieved August 18, 2011, from http://rockandice.com/component/content/article/37-tnb/1098-guys-weekend-and-the-third-day-on.

Blum, A. (2005). *Breaking Trail: A Climbing Life*. New York: Scribner.

BMC. (2006, May 27). "BMC Equity Survey Results." Retrieved from http://www.thebmc.co.uk/News.aspx?id=1030.

Bonatti, W. (2002). "Concepts of Adventure," in P. Ament (ed.), *Climber's Choice* (258–60). NY: Ragged Mountain Press.

Booth, D., & Thorpe, H. (2007) "The Meaning of Extreme," in *Berkshire Encyclopedia of Extreme Sports* (181–97). Great Barrington, MA: Berkshire Publishing.

Borden, I. (2001). *Skateboarding, Space and the City: Architecture and the Body*. Oxford, UK: Berg.

Bourdieu, P. (1977). *Outline of a Theory of Practice*. Cambridge, MA: Polity Press.

Boyd, J., & Munroe, K. J. (2003). "The Use of Imagery in Climbing." *Athletic Insight: The Online Journal of Sport Psychology* 5, no. 2, 15–30. Retrieved September 28, 2012, from http://www.athleticinsight.com/Vol5Iss2/ClimbingPDF.pdf.

Bridwell, J. (2003). "Brave New World," in A. Huber and H. Zak (eds.), *Yosemite: Half a Century of Dynamic Rock Climbing* (pp. 82–83). Birmingham, AL: Menasha Ridge Press.

Brindle, D., and Lewis, P. (2006, October 18). "Safety Last: Britons Urged to Cut Off the Cotton Wool and Rediscover Their Spirit of Adventure." *The Guardian* 3.

Bronski, P. (1996). "Who Were the Notorious Vulgarians?" *Traditional Mountaineering*. Retrieved June 20, 2009, from http://www.traditionalmountaineering.org/FAQ_Vulgarians.htm.

Browne, D. (2004). *Amped: How Big Air, Big Dollars, and a New Generation Took Sports to the Extreme*. London: Bloomsbury.

Buchroithner, A. (2010, November). "Entourage." *Urban Climber*, 6.

Burke, S., & Orlick, T. (2003). "Mental Strategies of Elite Mount Everest Climbers." *Journal of Excellence* 8, 42–58.

Burr, A. (2011, August). "Oasis: Old and New Classics in Utah's Lone Peak Cirque." *Climbing*, 56–63.

Cahall, F. (2010). "The King of Kings." *Climbing.com*. Retrieved July 17, 2011, from http://www.climbing.com/exclusive/features/threedegrees/index.html.

Cashmore, E. (2000). *Making Sense of Sports* (3rd ed.). London: Routledge.

Childs, G. (1998, September). "The Bird." *Climbing* 179, 74–81, 148–51.

Cliffhanger. (1993). Directed by Renny Harlin.

Climb. (2010). "Climbing 10 Times Safer than Football." 14.

ClimbandMore.com. (2007). "Dean Potter, b. 1972, USA." Retrieved May 3, 2010, from http://www.climbandmore.com/climbing,530,0,1,climbers.html.

Climber. (1997, May). "The Body Beautiful." 30–44.

Clune, R. (2010). "Fat City (510+) Shawngunks, New York." Retrieved June 10, 2011, from http://rockandice.com/articles/my-favorite-510/1171.

Codling, J. (1998). "The Walls, the Walls: A Punter's Guide." *On the Edge* 82, 52–53.

Coffey, M. (2003). *Fragile Edge: Loss on Everest*. London: Arrow Books.

Coffey, M. (2004). *Where the Mountain Casts Its Shadow: The Personal Costs of Climbing*. London: Arrow Books.

Connor, J. (2011, August). "King of the Cascades." *Climbing*, 64–69.

Dilley, R. (2007, August)."Women's Climbing Physicalities: Bodies, Experience and Representation." in V. Robinson, (ed.), "Gender and Extreme Sports: The Case of Climbing," special issue, *Sheffield Online Papers in Social Research* 10, 1–22

Donnelly, P. (2003). "Sports Climbing vs. Adventure Climbing," in R. E. Rinehart and S. Sydnor (eds.), *To the Extreme: Alternative Sports, Inside and Out* (291–304). Albany: SUNYP.

Donoso, T. (2011, April). "Higher Exposure: A Fresh Perspective on the Gunks." *Rock and Ice* 193, 38–42.

Dornian, D. (2003). "Xtreem." in R. E. Rinehart and S. Sydnor (eds.), *To The Extreme: Alternative Sports, Inside and Out* (281–90). Albany: State University of New York Press.

Douglas, E. (1999, July 29). "Packaged and Regulated, but Still Dangerous." *The Guardian*, p. 3.

Douglas, E. (2002, May). "Where There's a Hill." *Observer Magazine*, pp. 40–45.

Douglas, E. (2007, February 3). "Death in the Snow: Why Have Five Climbers Been Killed on One Peak?" *The Guardian*, p. 9.

Doyle, M. (2009, June). "Ultimate Strength: The Six-Week Guide to Long-term Gains." *Rock and Ice* 178, 60–63.

dpm. (2011). "Robyn Erbesfield-Raboutou Climbs Hard Boiled (V11)." Retrieved June 4, 2011, from http://www.dpmclimbing .com/articles/view/robyn-erbesfield-raboutou-climbs-hard-boiled-v11.

Duane, D. (1999, December). "Heroes: John Bachar." *Rock and Ice* 97, 68–79.

"Earth Science for Moorland School." (n.d.). Retrieved March 19, 2011, from http://www.moorlandschool.co.uk/earth/tectonic.htm.

Ellison, J. (2011, April). "Life on the Line: The Skinny on New Ropes," *Climbing*, 60–65.

Erbesfield-Raboutou, R. (2011). "Robyn Erbesfield-Raboutou." Retrieved September 23, 2011, from http://www.sportiva.com/ambassadors/ athletes/pro-climbing/robyn-erbesfield-raboutou.

Erickson, B. (2005). "Style Matters: Explorations of Bodies, Whiteness, and Identity in Rock Climbing." *Sociology of Sport Journal* 22, no. 3, 373–96.

Fallesen, G. (2011). "Raising Awareness: Recognizing Rock History in the Gunks." *Climbing for Christ*. Retrieved July 6, 2011, from http://www.climbingforchrist.org/Default.aspx?tabid=1459.

Fave, A. D., Bassi, M., & Massimini, F. (2003). "Quality of Experience and Risk Perception in High-Altitude Rock Climbing. *Journal of Applied Sport Psychology* 15, 82–98.

Fox, A. (2010). "Stohr Claims Second Female V13 Send." Retrieved September 27, 2010, from http://www.climbing.com/news/ hotflashes/stohr_claims_second_female_v13_send/.

Fox, A. (2011a). "Austrians Dominate Vail, Puccio Takes Second." *Climbing.com*. Retrieved September 26, 2011, from http://www .climbing.com/news/hotflashes/austrians_dominate_vail_puccio _takes_second/.

Fox, A. (2011b). "DiGiulian Wins Overall Gold at Arco." Retrieved September 28, 2011, from http://www.climbing.com/news/ hotflashes/digiulian_wins_overall_gold_at_arco/.

Fox, A. (2011c, April). "Harnesses." *Climbing*, 36–41.

Fox, A. (2011d, May). "Hot Flashes." *Climbing*, 14.

Fox, A. (2011e, August). "Hot Spots." *Climbing*, 24–29.

Fox, A. (2011f, March). "Off the Wall: Spring Migrations." *Climbing*, 20–21.

Fox, A. (2011g). "Playing the Game in Boulder Canyon." *Urban Climber Magazine*. Retrieved December 22, 2011, from http://www .urbanclimbermag.com/411/news/playing_the_game_in_boulder _canyon/.

Fox, A. (2011h, March). "Savoring the Spice: Pringle Unwraps a China Gem." *Climbing*, 16.

Fox, A. (2011i). "Sport Climbing Considered for 2020 Olympic Games." *Climbing.com*. Retrieved February 18, 2012, from http://www

.climbing.com/news/hotflashes/sport_climbing_considered_for_
2020_olympic_games/.

Fox Rogers, S. (1993, April/May). "Vulgarians Revisited." *Climbing* 137, 110–13, 161–62.

Fox Rogers, S. (2002). "Loose Woman," in P. Ament (ed.), *Climber's Choice* (262–67). New York: Ragged Mountain Press.

Franklin, M. (2009, June). "Whole Everything." *Rock and Ice* 178, 57.

Garlick, S. (2009). *Flakes, Jugs and Splitters: A Rock Climber's Guide to Geology*. Falcon Guides series. Globe Pequot Press.

Gear Guy. (2009, July). "White Goodness." *Rock and Ice* 179, 72.

Gear Guy. (2010, September). "Resurrecting Old Soles." *Rock and Ice* 188, 68–69.

Gear Guy. (2011, July). "Caught Crosswise." *Rock and Ice* 195, 76.

Geldard, J. (2008). "Beth Rodden—Meltdown—E11?" *UKClimbing.com*. Retrieved April 23, 2010 from http://www.ukclimbing.com/articles/page.php?id=864.

George, C. (2011, May). "Classic Climbs: The Headache." *Climbing*, 66.

Gifford, T. (1992). *John Muir: The Eight Wilderness-Discovery Books*. Seattle: The Mountaineers.

Gifford, T. (2004). *The Joy of Climbing: Terry Gifford's Classic Climbs*. Caithness, Scotland: Whittles Publishing.

Gifford, T. (2006). *Reconnecting with John Muir: Essays in Post-Pastoral Practice*. Athens: University of Georgia Press.

Godfrey, B., & Chelton, D. (1977). *Climb!: Rock Climbing in Colorado*. Boulder, CO: Alpine House Publishing.

Goodlad, B. (2005, June). "(Rock) Dancing Shoes." *Climber*, 68–70.

Grant, S., et al. (1996). "Anthropometric, Strength, Endurance and Flexibility Characteristics of Elite and Recreational Climbers." *Journal of Sports Sciences* 14, no. 4, 301–9.

Grant, S., et al. (2001). "A Comparison of the Anthropometric, Strength, Endurance and Flexibility Characteristics of Female Elite and Recreational Climbers and Non-climbers." *Journal of Sports Sciences* 19, 499–505.

Greene, G. (1998). "On the Rocks." *American Way* 31, no. 17, 44–49.

Gresham, N. (2009, June). "Ask the Coach." *Rock and Ice* 178, 68–69.

Griffith, J., Hart, C., Goodling, M., Kessler, J., & Whitmire, A. (2006). "Responses to the Sports Inventory for Pain among BASE Jumpers." *Journal of Sport Behavior* 29, 242–54.

Guthrie, J. (2010). "Kurt Albert (1/24/1954–9/28/2010)." Retrieved October 2, 2010, from http://www.climbing.com/community/perspective/kurt_albert/.

Harding, W. (2003). "El Capitan," in A. Huber and H. Zak (eds.), *Yosemite: Half a Century of Dynamic Rock Climbing* (pp. 44–49). Birmingham, AL: Menasha Ridge Press (Abridged from original article published 1959, *American Alpine Journal*).

Haston, S. (2010). "Stevie Haston Reviews Ron Fawcett's New Book." *UKClimbing.com*. Retrieved June 14, 2011, from http://www.ukclimbing.com/gear/review.php?id=2600.

Hill, L. (2002). *Climbing Free: My Life in the Vertical World*. New York: W.W. Norton and Company.

Hill, L. (2005). "Climbing and Responsibility." Retrieved August 5, 2011, from http://lynnhillclimbs.typepad.com/my_weblog/2005/04/climbing_and_re.html.

Hipshire, M. (2010, March). "Weight Up." *Rock and Ice* 184, 10–11.

Houlding, L. (2011, March). "The Prophet." *Rock and Ice* 192, 46–55.

Huber, A., & Zak, H. (eds.) (2003). *Yosemite: Half a Century of Dynamic Rock Climbing*. Birmingham, AL: Menasha Ridge Press.

IFSC. (2011). "Results and Rankings." Retrieved September 2, 2011, from http://www.ifsc-climbing.org/home.

Irvine, A. (2002). "The Path of Destruction," in P. Ament (ed.), *Climber's Choice* (200–203). New York: Ragged Mountain Press.

Jackson, J. (2009a). "Arc' teryx Harness Survey, 2007." *Rock and Ice*, Climbing Gear and Safety Guide, 18–24.

Jackson, J. (2009b, September). "Cliff Notes: Influence." *Rock and Ice* 180, 12.

Jackson, J. (2009c). "Hard Times." *Rock and Ice* 177, 10.

Jackson, J. (2009d). "Rock and Ice B.I.G. Awards." *Rock and Ice* 177. 14–16.

Jackson, J. (2010a). "Zen and the Art of Wife Maintenance." Retrieved September 29, 2010, from http://rockandice.com/component/content/article/37-tnb/1154-zen-and-the-art-of-wife-maintenance.

Jackson, J. (2010b). "Cold Blooded." Retrieved August 31, 2010, from http://www.facebook.com/note.php?note_id=435547327816.

Jackson, J. (2010c, September). "Yosemite's Lost Film: Never-Before-Seen Images from the Golden Era." *Rock and Ice* 188, 36–41.

Jackson, J. (2010d, July). "The Cobra Den: Bollywood Adventure and Jungle Critters in South India." Rock and Ice 187, 36–47, 74–76.

Jackson, J. (2011a, March). "Be Like Leo." *Rock and Ice* 192, 8.

Jackson, J. (2011b, June). "The Greatest Climber of All Time." *Rock and Ice* 194, 10.

Jackson, J. (2011c, July). "Ropes Don't Break—They Cut." *Rock and Ice* 195, 22.

Jenkins, M. (2011, May). "Yosemite Climbers." *National Geographic*, 98–117.

Jones, C. (1997). *Climbing in North America.* Seattle, WA: The Mountaineers.

Kay, J., & Laberge, S. (2003). "Imperialistic Construction of Freedom in Warren Miller's *Freeriders*," in R. Rinehart and S. Sydnor (eds.), *To the Extreme: Alternative Sports, Inside and Out* (381–400). Albany: State University of New York Press.

Kern, S. (2011, May). "Ondra: Face to Face with the World's Best Climber." *Urban Climber*, 56–65.

Kiewa, J. (2001). " 'Stepping around Things': Gender Relationships in Climbing." *Australian Journal of Outdoor Education* 5, no. 2, 4–12.

Kinder, J. (2010, September). "What I've Learned." *Rock and Ice* 188, 32.

King Huber, N., & Roller, J. A. (2004). "Bedrock Geology of the Yosemite Valley Area, Yosemite National Park, California." *USGS.com*. Retrieved November 4, 2011, from http://geomaps.wr.usgs.gov/parks/yos/I_1639.html

Kirkpatrick, M. (1997, May). "Obsession." *Climber*, 78.

Klimt, E. (2010, April). "Everybody Does Fall." *Rock and Ice* 185, 12.

Kogan, N., & M. A. Wallach (1964). *Risk Taking: A Study in Cognition and Personality*. Oxford, England: Holt, Rinehart & Winston.

Koukoubis, T. D., Cooper, L. W., Glisson, R. R., Seaber, A. V., & Feagin, J. A. Jr. (1995). "An Electromyographic Study of Arm Muscles during Climbing." *Knee Surgery, Sports Traumatology, Arthroscopy* 3, no. 2, 121–24.

Kroese, M. (2001). *Fifty Favorite Climbs: The Ultimate North American Tick List*. Seatle, WA: The Mountaineers Books.

Lash, S. (1993). "Reflexive Modernization: The Aesthetic Dimension." *Theory, Culture and Society* 10, 1–23.

Lash, S. (2000). "Risk Culture," in B. Adams, U. Beck, and J. Van Loon (eds.), *The Risk Society and Beyond* (47–62) London: Sage.

Laurendeau, J. (2006). "He didn't Go in Doing A Skydive": Sustaining the Illusion of Control in an Edgework Activity, *Sociological Perspectives* 49, No. 4, 583–605.

Laviolette, P. (2007). "Hazardous Sport?" *Anthropology Today* 23, no. 6, 1–2.

Lipinski, D. (2011, April 17/18).What Adam Ondra Means for the Sport of Climbing, *Mountains and Water.com*. Retrieved September 11, 2011 from http://www.mountainsandwater.com/search?q=what+adam+ondra+means

Llewellyn, D., et al. (2008). "Self-efficacy, Risk Taking and Performance in Rock Climbing." *Personality and Individual Differences* 45, 75–81.

Llewellyn, D. J., & Sanchez, X. (2007). "Individual Differences and Risk Taking in Rock Climbing." *Psychology of Sport and Exercise* 9, no. 4, 413–26.

Long, J., & Fidelman, D. (2009). *The Stonemasters: California Rock Climbers in the Seventies*. Costa Mesa, CA: T. Adler Books/Stonemaster Press.

Loomis, M. (2011, August). "Southern Exposure: Four Classic Ways to Beat the Crowds on the Grand Teton." *Climbing*, 16–20.

Lowell, J. (1999, December). "Monkeyin' Around: Chris Sharma's Blissful Romp through American Bouldering." *Rock and Ice* 97, 87–91.

Lowell, J. (2009, September). "New York Stories: Bouldering in the Big Apple and Beyond." *Rock and Ice* 180, 51.

Lucas, J. (2011, January). "Generational Shift: The New Faces of Tuolumne Climbing." *Rock and Ice* 191, 58–65.

Luebben, C. (1999, December). "Heroes: Layton Kor." *Rock and Ice* 97, 68–79.

Lynch, D. (2009, July). "Average Superstar." *Rock and Ice* 179, 11.

Lyng, S. (1990). "Edgework: A Social Psychological Analysis of Voluntary Risk-taking." *American Journal of Sociology* 95, 851–86.

Lyng, S. (2005). "Edgework and the Risk-Taking Experience," in S. Lyng (ed.), *Edgework: The Sociology of Risk-Taking* (17–49). London: Routledge.

MacDonald, D. (1999, December). "Heroes." *Rock and Ice* 97, 12.

MacDonald, D. (2007). "Astroman and Rostrum Free-Solo." *Climbing*. Retrieved November 21, 2010, from http://www.climbing.com/news/hotflashes/yosemitesolos07/.

MacDonald, D. (2008). "Erbesfield-Raboutou: 5.14a at Age 45." *Climbing*. Retrieved January 10, 2010, from http://www.climbing.com/news/hotflashes/erbesfield_raboutou_514a_at_age_45/.

MacDonald, D. (2010). "Kurt Albert Dead at 56." Retrieved October 2, 2010, from http://www.urbanclimbermag.com/411/news/kurt_albert_dead_at_56/.

MacDonald, D. (2011a, March). "More Is Better: More Destinations, More Gear." *Climbing*, 10.

MacDonald, D. (2011b, February/March). "The Latest." *Urban Climber*, 26–27.

Maguire, J. (1999.) *Global Sport: Identities, Societies, Civilizations.* Cambridge, MA: Polity.

Maley, J. (2006, June 9). "Italians Passed Us By, Says Everest Rescuer." *The Guardian.*

MarcC. (2009). "Re: Should Lost City Routes Be Added to rc.com?" *Gunks.com*. Retrieved January 8, 2010, from http://gunks.com/ubbthreads7/ubbthreads.php/topics/47956/MarcC#Post47956.

Mazel, D. (1991). *Pioneering Ascents: The Origins of Climbing in America, 1642–1873.* Harrisburg, PA: Stackpole Books.

McClure, S. (2009). "Great Britons." Retrieved August 3, 2011 from http://www.ukclimbing.com/articles/page.php?id=1968/.

Mcinerney, C. (2011, February/March). "Natural Born Drillers." *Urban Climber*, 38–45.

Mellor, D. (2001). *American Rock: Region, Rock and Culture in American Climbing.* Woodstock, VT: The Country Man Press.

Mermier, C. M., Robergs, R. A., McMinn, S. M., & Heyward, V. H. (1997). "Energy Expenditure and Physiological Responses during Indoor Rock Climbing." *British Journal of Sports Medicine* 31, 224–28.

Messner, M., et al. (1999). *Boys to Men, Sports Media: Messages about Masculinity*. Oakland, CA: Children Now.

Meyers, G. (ed.). (1979). *Yosemite Climber*. Modesto, CA: Robbins Mountain Letters.

Midol, N., & Broyer, G. (1995). "Toward an Anthropological Analysis of New Sport Cultures: The Case of Whiz Sports in France." *Society of Sport Journal* 12, 204–12.

Moffatt, J. (2003). "Bouldering," in A. Huber and H. Zak (eds.), *Yosemite: Half a Century of Dynamic Rock Climbing* (pp. 100–6). Birmingham, AL: Menasha Ridge Press.

Ondra, A. (2011). "Personal Profile." *8a.nu*. Retrieved July 20, 2011, from http://www.8a.nu/?IncPage=http%3A//www.8a.nu/user/Profile. aspx%3FUserId%3D1476.

Osius, A. (2009a, October). "Thanks for the Dreams." *Rock and Ice* 181, 24.

Osius, A. (2009b). "Ties That Bind: Tips for Selecting Your Precious Cord." *Rock and Ice*. Climbing Gear and Safety Guide, 177, 24–36.

Osius, A. (2010, October). "Cliff Notes." *Rock and Ice*, 189, 18–20.

Oxlade, C. (2003). *Extreme Sports: Rock Climbing*. Minneapolis, MN: LernerSports.

Palmer, C. (2004). "Death, Danger and the Selling of Risk in Adventure Sports," in B. Wheaton (ed.), *Understanding Lifestyle Sports: Consumption, Identity and Difference* (55–69). London: Routledge.

Persson, P. (2010, April). "Shame on You." *Rock and Ice* 185, 14.

Peters, A. (2011, May). "Road Trips: American Classics: Colorado, Routing Done Right." *Urban Climber*, 38–47.

PlanetMountain.com. (2009, February 16). "Jerry Moffatt Interview." Retrieved February 10, 2010, from http://www.planetmountain .com/english/News/shownews1.lasso?keyid=36598.

Plate, K. R. (2007, August). "Rock Climbing Is a Masculine Sport? Understanding the Complex Gendered Subculture of Rock Climbing," in V. Robinson (ed.), "Gender and Extreme Sports: The Case of Climbing," special issue of *Sheffield Online Papers in Social Research* 10, 1–14.

PlateTectonics.com. (2010). "Plate Boundaries." Retrieved June 18, 2011, from http://www.platetectonics.com/book/page_5.asp.

prAna. (2010). "Dean Potter." Retrieved August 21, 2011, from http://www.prana.com/ambassadors/dean-potter.

Pratt, C. (2002). "The South Face of Mount Watkins," in P. Ament (ed.), *Climber's Choice* (50–61). New York: Ragged Mountain Press.

Raleigh, D. (2009a, October). "The One: Bachar's Enduring Legacy." *Rock and Ice* 181, 56–57.

Raleigh, D. (2009b). "Rock and Ice B.I.G. Awards." *Rock and Ice* 177, 14–16.

Raleigh, D (2010a, September 21). "Alone on El Cap." *Rock and Ice.* Retrieved September 24, 2010, from http://rockandice.com/tnb-blog/alone-on-el-cap.html?blogger=Duane+Raleigh.

Raleigh, D. (2010b). "95 5.13s and Counting." *Rock and Ice.* Retrieved November 25, 2010, from http://rockandice.com/news/1240-95-513s-and-counting.

Reel Rock Tour (2011). Retrieved February 20, 2012, http://outdoor.nmsu.edu/aas/reelrock.html.

Reith, G. (1999). "On the Edge: Drugs and the Consumption of Risk in Late Modernity," in S. Lyng (ed.), *Edgework: The Sociology of Risk-Taking* (227–245). London: Routledge.

Rickaby, K. (2005, June). "New Gear." *Climber*, 66–67.

Rinehart, R., & Sydnor, S. (2003). "Proem," in R. Rinehart and S. Sydnor (eds.), *To the Extreme: Alternative Sports, Inside and Out* (1–17). Albany: State University of New York Press.

Robbins, R. (2003). "North America Wall," in A. Huber and H. Zak (eds.), *Yosemite: Half a Century of Dynamic Rock Climbing* (pp. 62–66). Birmingham, AL: Menasha Ridge Press.

Robbins, R. (2002). "Jack of Diamonds" in P. Ament (ed.), *Climber's Choice* (pp. 63–69). NY: Ragged Mountain Press.

Robinson, D. (2009, October). "The Gift: The Rise and Transformation of John Bachar." *Rock and Ice* 181, 58.

Robinson, V. (2008). *Everyday Masculinities and Extreme Sport: Male Identity and Rock Climbing*. Oxford: Berg.

Rock and Ice. (1999, December). "Heroes." *Rock and Ice* 97, 78.

Rockclimbing.com. (2011). "Auburn State Recreation Area." Retrieved September 23, 2011, from http://www.rockclimbing.com/routes/

North_America/United_States/California/Sacramento_Area/
Auburn_State_Recreation_Area/.

Rodden, B. (2009). "What I've Learned." *Rock and Ice*. Retrieved October 10, 2010, from http://rockandice.com/articles/what-ive -learned/article/827-beth-rodden.

Rooks, M. D. (1997, April). "Rock Climbing Injuries." *Sports Medicine* 23, no. 4, 261–70.

Roper, S. (1994). *Camp 4: Recollections of a Yosemite Rockclimber*. London: Baton Wicks.

Roper, S., & Steck, A. (1997). *Fifty Classic Climbs of North America. San Francisco*, CA: Sierra Club Books.

Rose, M. B., & Parsons, M. C. (2002). *Invisible on Everest: Innovation and the Gear Makers*. Philadelphia: Old City Publishing.

Ryan, M. (2005, April). "Climb Like a Girl. Part 1." *UKClimbing.com*. Retrieved August 17, 2012, from http://www.ukclimbing.com/ articles/page.php?id=107.

Ryan, M. (2008). "Election Day Blues: Bolts Smashed in the USA." *UKClimbing.com*. Retrieved August 10, 2009, from http://www .ukclimbing.com/news/item.php?id=45422.

Sarrazin, P., Roberts, G. C., Cury, F., Biddle, S., & Famose, J. P. (2002). "Exerted Effort and Performance in Climbing among Boys: The Influence of Achievement Goals, Perceived Ability, and Task Difficulty." *Research Quarterly for Exercise & Sport* 73, no. 4, 425–36.

Saunders, J. (2010, June). "Ask Dr. J." *Rock and Ice* 186, 72–75.

Saunders, J. (2011, March). "Ask Dr. J." *Rock and Ice* 192, 70.

SCC. (2010). "Lisa Rands Interview." Retrieved July 5, 2011, from http:// www.seclimbers.org/modules.php?name=News&file=article &sid=249.

Scheinbaum, C. (2011, May). "Road Trips: American Classics: Naturally Northeast, Climbing in the Colonies." *Urban Climber*, 38–47.

Schwartz, S. E. B. (1993, April/May). "True Gunk." *Climbing* 137, 100–9.

Scully, L. (2010, January). "Routes Less Traveled." *Rock and Ice* 183, 40–46.

Segal, M. (2010, November). "Escape Route: Finding Solace in the Sawtooths." *Rock and Ice* 190, 44–51.

Shepherd, N. (1998, August/September). "Royal Robbins." *On the Edge*, 38–45.

Sherman, J. (1994). *Stone Crusade: A Historical Guide to Bouldering in America*. Golden, CO: The American Alpine Club.

Sherman, J. (1999). *Sherman Exposed: Slightly Censored Climbing Stories*. Seattle, WA: The Mountaineers.

Siegrist, J. (2010). "History of American Sport Climbing." *Climbing*. Retrieved January 2, 2011, from http://www.climbing.com/photo-video/gallery/history_of_american_sport_climbing/.

Siegrist, J. (2011, May). "What Happens in Vegas . . . Will Keep You in Vegas." *Urban Climber*, 48–55.

Smart, B. (2005). *The Sport Star: Modern Sport and the Cultural Economy of Sporting Celebrity*. London: Sage.

Smith, C. W. (2005). "Financial Edgework: Trading in Market Currents," in S. Lyng (ed.), *Edgework: The Sociology of Risk-Taking*. (187–200). London: Routledge.

Smith, K. (2011). "Older and Stronger: Age Can't Stop Canada's Female Climbers." *Gripped: The Climbing Magazine*. Retrieved February 12, 2012, from http://gripped.com/2011/04/sections/articles/older-stronger/.

Smith, M. (2000). "The Science of Climbing and Mountaineering." January, *Australian Journal of Outdoor Education* 4, No, 2.

Smith, N. (2010, January). "Wild West Virginia: Seneca Rocks." *Climbing* 183, 48–55.

Snider, L. (2009, June). "Too Thin to Win?" *Rock and Ice* 178, 55–56.

Snider, L. (2011, May). "Go Green: What to Do with Your Old Gear." *Climbing*, 22.

Stephens, D. (2010, July). "Borderline." *Rock and Ice* 187, 10.

Stirling, S. (2009). "Mountaineering Mums." *UKClimbing.com*. Retrieved September 27, 2009, from http://www.ukclimbing.com/articles/page.php?id=1739.

Stoppler, M. C., & Shiel, W. C. (2007). "Endorphins: Natural Pain and Stress Fighters." *MedicineNet.com*. Retrieved June 25, 2011 from http://www.medicinenet.com/script/main/art.asp?articlekey=55001.

Stranger, L. (1999). "The Aesthetics of Risk': A Study of Surfing." *International Review for the Sociology of Sport* 34, no. 3, 265–76.

Summers, K. (2007, August). "Unequal Genders: Mothers and Fathers on Mountains," in V. Robinson (ed.), "Gender and Extreme Sports: The Case of Climbing," special issue *Sheffield Online Papers in Social Research* 10, 1–15.

Tejada-Flores, L. (1997). "Foreword," in C. Jones, *Climbing in North America* (7–8). Seattle, WA: The Mountaineers.

Than, K. (2006). "Taller Mountains Blamed on Global Warming, Too." Retrieved March 4, 2011, from http://www.livescience.com/938-taller-mountains-blamed-global-warming.html Thornburg, J. (2009, June). "Tuff Love." *Rock and Ice* 178, 38–43.

Thorpe, H. (2010). "Bourdieu, Gender Reflexivity and Physical Culture: A Case of Masculinities in the Snowboarding Field." *Journal of Sport and Social Issues* 34, no. 2, 176–214.

Tower, A. (2011) "Mexican Mischief at the 2010 Petzl RocTrip." Urban Climber. February/March), 46–51.

Tulloch, J., & Lupton, D. (2003). *Risk and Everyday Life*. London: Sage.

Urban Climber. (2010). "The Booty Matrix." *Urban Climber*, 44.

Urban Climber. (2011a, April). "Harnesses: The Key to Happiness." *Urban Climber*, 32–36.

Urban Climber. (2011b, April). "Ropes: The Key to Happiness." *Urban Climber*, 38–43.

Urban Climber. (2011c, February/March). "The 2010 Urby Awards." *Urban Climber*, 52–58.

Utah Geological Survey. (2011). "What Are Igneous, Sedimentary, & Metamorphic Rocks?" Retrieved February 19, 2012, from http://geology.utah.gov/surveynotes/gladasked/gladrocks.htm.

Van Leuven, C., and Summit, C. (2011, May) "Road Trips: American Classics: Classic California, Navigating the West Coast of Climbing." *Urban Climber*, 38–47.

Van Middlebrook, J. (2010, March). "Warrior's Way." *Rock and Ice* 184, 12.

Vause, M. (1997). "Knights of Nothingness: The Transcendental Nature of Mountaineering and Mountain Literature." *The Himalayan Journal* 53, 1–14.

Vomáčko, S. (2005). "The Influence of Selected Factors on the Performance of Sport Climbers," in Jiří Baláš, Ondřej Pohanka, and Ladislav Vomáčko (eds.), *Proceedings from 2nd International Mountain and Outdoor Sports Conference* (pp. 86–95). Hruba Skala, Czech Republic.

Warnock, L. (2011, May). "Road Trips: American Classics: The Dirty South, Best Bouldering in the US." *Urban Climber*, 38–47.

Waterman, L., and Waterman, G. (1993). *Yankee Rock and Ice: A History of Climbing in the North Eastern United States*. Mechanicsburg, PA: Stackpole.

Watters, R. (2003). "The Wrong Side of the Thin Edge," in R. Rinehart and S. Sydnor (eds.), *To The Extreme: Alternative Sports, Inside and Out* (257–266). Albany: State University of New York Press.

Watts, P. B., Daggett, M., Gallagher, P., & Wilkins, B. (2000). "Metabolic Response during Sport Rock Climbing and the Effects of Active versus Passive Recovery." *International Journal of Sports Medicine* 21, no. 3, 185–90.

Watts, P. B., Martin, D., & Durtschi, S.(1993). "Anthropometric Profiles of Elite Male and Female Competitive Sport Rock Climbers." *Journal of Sports Sciences* 11, no. 2, 113–17.

Webster, E. (1999, December). "Heroes: Fritz Weissner." *Rock and Ice* 97, 68–79.

Weidner, C. (2011, April). "Sweet Shoes." *Climbing*, Gear Guide, 66–73.

Wells, C. (2001). *A Brief History of British Mountaineering*. Nottingham, Nottinghamshire, UK: The Mountain Heritage Trust.

Wheaton, B. (2000). " 'New Lads'? Masculinities and the 'New Sport' Participant." *Men and Masculinities Journal* 2, no. 4, 434–56.

Wheaton, B. (ed.). (2004). *Understanding Lifestyle Sports: Consumption, Identity and Difference*. London: Routledge.

Wheaton, B. (2007). "After Sport Culture: Rethinking Sport and Post-Subcultural Theory." *Journal of Sport and Social Issues* 31, no. 3, 283–307.

Wilson, K. (2007). *Classic Rock: Great British Rock Climbs* (2nd ed.). London: Baton Wicks Publications.

Woods, A. (2010). "More Hard Ascents at Lincoln Lake." *Climbing*. Retrieved April 4, 2011, from http://www.climbing.com/news/hotflashes/more_hard_ascents_at_lincoln_lake/.

Woods, D. (2010). "About." *Daniel Woods Blog.* Retrieved September 4, 2011, from http://danielwoods.us/.

Woods, D. (2011). "Personal Profile." *8a.nu.* Retrieved September 8, 2011, from http://www.8a.nu/?IncPage=http%3A//www.8a.nu/user/Profile.aspx%3FUserId%3D4102.

Woodward, K. (2002). *Understanding Identity.* London: Arnold.

Wright, D. M., Royle, T. J., & Marshall, T. (2001). "Indoor Rock Climbing: Who Gets Injured?" *British Journal of Sports Medicine* 35, no. 3, 181–85.

Wright, R. M. (2009, June). "The Superior Strategy." *Rock and Ice* 178, 68–69.

Yates, S. (2002). *The Flame of Adventure.* London: Vintage.

Young, J. (2009). "The Access Fund: Foresight and Follow-Through." *RockClimbing.com.* Retrieved November 12, 2011, from http://www.rockclimbing.com/Articles/Climbing_History_and_Trivia/The_Access_Fund_Foresight_and_Follow-Through_949.html.

Zuckerman, M. (2000). "Are You a Risk Taker?" *Psychology Today.* Retrieved July 17, 2011, from http://www.psychologytoday.com/articles/200011/are-you-risk-taker.

Zuckerman, M., & Kuhlman, D. M.(2000). "Personality and Risk-Taking: Common Bisocial Factors." *Journal of Personality* 68, no. 6, 999–1029.

index

Note: Terms that are italicized refer to actual climbs and geographical areas in the United States, and elsewhere, mentioned in this book.

about the author

VICTORIA ROBINSON, PhD, is a reader in sociology at the University of Sheffield, UK. Her research interests are in extreme sport (particularly rock climbing), gender and sexualities, and men and masculinities. She is the author of *Everyday Masculinities: Male Identity and Rock Climbing* (2008), *Mundane Heterosexualities: From Theory to Practices* (2007, with J. Hockey and A. Meah), and *Masculinities in Transition* (2011, with J. Hockey). She is coeditor, with D. Richardson, of the third edition of *Introducing Gender and Women's Studies* (2008), as well as Palgrave's international book series *Genders and Sexualities in the Social Sciences*. Currently she is writing a chapter on methods for researching masculinity and male climbers, and another on new directions in "extreme leisure" for Routledge's *The Handbook of Leisure Studies*. She lives with her son, Fast Eddie Joe Robinson, age 18, in Sheffield, UK, close to the gritstone.